The Power of
Psychic Awareness

The Power of Psychic Awareness

Kingdon L. Brown

PARKER PUBLISHING COMPANY, INC.
West Nyack, N.Y.

Reward Edition . . . . . November, 1973

This book is a reference work based on research by
the author. The opinions expressed herein are not
necessarily those of or endorsed by the Publisher.

Dedicated to Almeda,
who understood these truths
before they were articulated.

HOW THIS BOOK
CAN HELP YOU

Is it possible to change your life for greater fulfillment of your desires?

Yes, it is most certainly possible! Most people would be satisfied to change only a few things. A frustrating situation here. A disturbing element there. *But, there is a way to change the very core of your existence for the better.*

This book gives you ways and means for getting psychic awareness—complete with easy to perform programs and techniques that will enable you to reach your highest and best human potentials. Why? Because life itself is an ordered process. It operates according to predictable principles. These principles or laws govern the human spirit in all of us. When you understand the dynamic laws of your own psychic self—you can direct your life toward your most cherished fulfillment.

You will get to know where you stand in the total scheme of all things. Harmony, peace, healing, prosperity and knowledge of powerful psychic forces can now be yours for your own use. You tap the hidden power of your own spirit. And this new-found power will order your life in the same way it orders the universe—by unfailing, predictable application of omnipotent principle. It is simply a matter of your knowing what those principles are and how to use them.

The problem most students of mysticism first encounter is that the working techniques for reaching this greater cosmo-psychic awareness are almost non-existent. The techniques that may be available are complicated. Some of them are too time-consuming. Others from mystic sources are entirely foreign and confusing to the Western or "modern" mind.

In this volume are presented programed methods that you will easily understand—and through the practice of which you can soon develop your own higher and constructive mental abilities. Your religious affiliation does not matter; neither does your occupation or social background. You can use what you read in this book. You can put it into practice immediately. You will learn of the satisfying experiences of others in the case histories in this book.

A complete system of attaining psychic awareness is set out for you. The only demands this system makes is that you have some available time and that you use that time as this book guides you for one of the greatest experiences in your life.

The refreshing difference of the psychic awareness method in this book is that you are taken along the psychic path, step by step, in such a way that brings certain mastery of the art of psychic awareness. It is a systematic process, and it is not mysterious to the point of incredibility. It is a carefully planned development of the capacities *already within you!* You will gain firm control over every aspect of your life. You will no longer be a victim of fate pushed from place to place by events or causes not of your own making. You will overcome the shadows of the past, and you will be shown how to use psychic mechanisms every day in any situation. You will be able to attract the "right" people, circumstances, and opportunities to change your life most definitely for the better.

All this is not a matter of simply adjusting one's self to the world, or merely reducing your tensions. It is not claimed that the effects of an uncoordinated life can be automatically eradicated by convincing one's self that it simply does not exist. The process given you in this book is one of continuous growth in awareness—one of the great secrets of a successfully fulfilled life.

Through the programs in helping yourself, and the experiences of others in this book, you will be able to locate your own true self, your own psychic expression, your own power and dominion over this life as YOU want to live it.

Kingdon L. Brown

CONTENTS

1. Cosmo-Psychic Universe **15**

Life Cycles and the Planes of Existence
The Doorways to Psychic Awareness
Basic Meditational Methods
Harmony and Healing
Clairvoyant Understanding
Casting Forward in Time
Prosperity and Business Success
Love and Intuition
Self-Improvement and Originality
Points to Remember from This Chapter

2. How to Be Guided Through Your Extra-Sensory Impressions **37**

What Is an Impression?
Where Do Extra-Sensory Impressions Come from?
Some Ordinary and Not So Ordinary E. S. P.
What Do Impressions Say?
How to Interpret Impressions
Basic Techniques in Developing
    Extra-Sensory Perception
Space-Line Exercises
Time-Line Exercises
Will Extra-Sensory Perception Change
    Your Way of Life?
Beginning the Six-Fold Daily Plan
    of Extra-Sensory Perception Exercises
Your E. S. P. Meditation Outline
Points to Remember from This Chapter

3. **How to Attract the Right People and Things for Your Benefit** **63**

*Guidance and Direction from
    the Superconscious
Release and Give Your Super-
    conscious a Chance
Repelling Negation
Looking for the Positive
The Positive Use of Negation
Creating the Future Ahead of Time
How to Set Lasting Goals
Syndrome Creation in the Cosmos
How to Avoid Repeating Damaging
    Past Experiences
Love Is the Magic Ingredient
Exercises to Perform
Points to Remember from This Chapter*

4. **How Cosmic Law Operates and What It Does for You** **85**

*Putting Cosmic Law to Work
How to Expand
Two Forces Operating in the Universe?
Directing the Entire Force
    of Your Being
Protection from Unwanted Influences
Your Personal Inventory
Your Life Cycle
Your Inner World Influences
    the Outer World
Activation
The Now Moment of Self-Realization
Exercises to Perform
Points to Remember from This Chapter*

5. **How to Live the Life You Want Through Psychic Illumination** **111**

*The Characteristics of Complete
    Cosmic Illumination
The Royal Road to Complete
    Cosmic Illumination*

5. How to Live the Life You Want Through Psychic Illumination (*cont.*)

*How to Meditate for Complete
   Cosmic Illumination*
First Week
Second Week
Third Week
Meditational Tips
*The Five Intellectual Realizations
   in Cosmic Illumination*
*Acceptance, Rejection, and Realization
   in Cosmic Illumination*
How to Reject
What to Accept
When to Realize
*How to Regulate Your Destiny with
   Complete Cosmic Illumination*
*Something Else You Can Expect from
   Complete Cosmic Illumination*
Exercises to Perform
Points to Remember from This Chapter

6. Self-Realization Awareness Through Sleep, Dreams, and Trance **135**

How to Program Your Sleep
What Your Dream Symbols Mean
Using Your Dream Diary
What Is Self-Realization?
How to Encourage Dreaming
When Not to Sleep
*Trance, Automatic Writing, and Astral
   Projection*
The Trance Theory
Exercises to Perform
Points to Remember from This Chapter

7. How to Communicate with Those Who Have Passed On **159**

Mediumship and World Events
Mediumship Begins
What Is a Medium?

7. How to Communicate with Those Who Have Passed On (*cont.*)

Predictions of Future Events
How to Develop Mediumship
Nine Fundamentals of Spirit Communication
First Steps in Psychic Sensitivity
Your Inner Band and Your Outer Band
What Happens to Spirit Beings?
Finding a Development Group
Receiving Spirit in a Development Group
Verifying Messages
Interpretation
Building the Vibration
Questioning the Guides, for Sure
When Not to Communicate
Exercises to Perform
Points to Remember from This Chapter

8. How to Protect Yourself from Psychic Attack . . . 179

*Three Classic Cases of Malicious Psychic
    Attack*
Symptoms of Malicious Psychic Attack
The Metaphysical Protection Theory
Diagnosis of Malicious Psychic Attack
Reversing Malicious Psychic Attacks
*The Ethics of Reversing Malicious
    Psychic Attack*
Protective Conditioning
*Protective Affirmation to Ward Off
    Bodily Harm*
*Protective Affirmation to Ward Off
    Mental Harm*
*Protective Affirmation to Ward Off
    Spiritual Harm*
*Protective Affirmation to Ward Off
    Financial Disaster*
*Protective Affirmation to Ward Off
    Disturbing Relationships*
Exercises to Perform
Points to Remember from This Chapter

The Power of
Psychic Awareness

This book is about a miracle. That miracle is you and your higher powers of mind.

You are the star in the story we are about to tell because by the time you have closed this

1

The Cosmo-Psychic Universe and Your Exciting Place in It

book you will have the keys to a vital and dynamic life adventure. We will start with you as you are now. Then, we'll show you how to use what you already have, *your psychic awareness* and your dynamic mental power, in the creation of an energy-infused life, a life transformed by cosmic attunement.

It will begin with a search. A search for the truth of your being. Along the way, you'll find yourself formulating answers to such basic questions as: Who are you? Where are you headed? And, of course, are you getting where you want to go?

Through case histories, theory, and practical technique, you'll learn how to attune yourself to the cosmos, to the universe, and all the fascinating creativity that is there. This creativity is reflected in you. Your full psychic awareness is waiting, at this very moment, whether you realize it or not, to be tapped for *your* benefit. After reading this book, you'll be able to duplicate the same marvelous results that other people, just like yourself, have produced with no more "raw material" than you have right now. You'll start with some basic exercises in mental and emotional conditioning. You'll see results in your life that will amaze you and your friends. Then you'll graduate to higher and higher level perceptions, insights, and achievements. Eventually you will be using your psychic awareness and cosmic attunement quite naturally. You won't be amazed anymore, but you will be quite pleased and delighted.

Some case histories in point

"Who is that man in your living room?" a young lady asked me as she entered my study for a consultation. .

"His name is Matthew," I said. "Why?"

"He is the most attractive man I've ever seen. He glows with masculinity and sex appeal," she said with a wink.

Matthew was a student of psychic awareness. He was an excellent student who was realizing his true place in the cosmos. If this same young lady had seen him a year earlier she wouldn't have looked at him twice—for then his inner discord, mental wanderings, and hateful attitude made his appearance dull and commonplace.

A year after this woman had seen the gentleman in my living room, she too had a radiance and zest for living that showed in her face and eyes as a magnetic power. She, in the meantime, had begun her own development of awareness, awareness of herself, other people, and the world. Her affection for every single person was genuine. She had become outgoing because she found a true understanding of herself and her exciting place in the universe.

How Bertram Got Theatrical Success

Bertram was a motion picture exhibitor. That is, he owned several first-run theaters where he showed films distributed by major producers. He was in keen competition with several other exhibitors who bid against him for permission to show new films in their theaters.

After a lecture on psychic awareness Bertram called me and made an appointment. His request of me was direct. "My business is in terrible shape. I need a winner, just one good picture would be enough to get me going again. My financial position is shaky, can you do anything to help?" he asked.

"I can teach you how to know what hidden forces are at work. Through increased awareness of these forces you can practically live a charmed life. If you want to be a successful showman I can teach you how to teach yourself to be one," I replied.

We began simple exercises for increased personal awareness. Several months later Bertram bid on a "sleeper"—a picture that most exhibitors ignored. It opened in one of his theaters as a smash hit which broke all records. It put him on the map as a major exhibitor again who knew how to promote films and get *big* box office!

Bertram attributed his success to his increased awareness of those influences which are moving, all the time, underneath the surface. It was his own insight that caused him to "buy" this winning film after having seen it at a private screening. The other exhibitors turned thumbs down on it since its content was controversial. But, Bertram went for it and his gamble paid off handsomely.

How a Plain Spinster Gained Glamor

Agnes was a lackluster spinster who worked as a public stenographer. She was always correct and unbending. So correct and so unbending that she probably scared off any men who might have been interested in her.

She had some spare time and undertook a study of psychic awareness and cosmic attunement. She found that some rather serious, fragmented and discordant thoughts were holding her back and blocking her fulfillment as a human being.

Through her understanding of her true place in the cosmos, in the total scheme of things, she gradually blossomed into a lovely, warm person with more charm and personality

Agnes' new found personality not only made her more successful in her business but it brought new friendships and eventually a proposal of marriage. She was delighted. Today, she is happily married, a fine person with an excellent character. She told me privately that she was as shocked as anyone else when she received her marriage proposal.

"I'd become so accustomed to being single that I never thought it would happen," she said. "I guess I was preparing myself for it by studying greater awareness even though I didn't realize it at the time."

A College Student's Clairvoyance

Dolly, a college student in her early twenties, developed clairvoyance as a result of increasing her awareness and finding her place in the cosmos. She was able to foretell events with amazing accuracy. A friend of hers was able to exert a healing and reconciling force as a result of her increased awareness and receptivity to cosmic influences.

Life, it seems, is a series of experiences, or phases, through which we pass in order to grow and develop.

Life cycles and the planes of existence

Only the experience of our higher faculties of mind can convince us that we are more than just physical bodies. However, the following assumptions about our origin and nature, and the general course of life, will help to explain what takes place. The exact proof for the validity of these assumptions will come to you, gradually, as you wrestle with the problems of your own life and as you are able to test and consider reality and your exciting place in the cosmos.

Here are the cycles and planes:

1. We are born with a spiritual component, our soul, which comes to us as a portion of the God-Power. This divinity within can be tapped and utilized as a power source of infinite creativity.

2. As life progresses, in approximately seven-year cycles, we have opportunities to learn how to experience the operation of this divine power.

3. When we leave the encumbrance of the body at death our soul moves to another plane of existence or another state of consciousness.

4. The plane of existence where we adjust to our new condition of spirituality can be called the *astral* plane of consciousness.

5. We continue to grow and develop in the astral plane until we reach a more *ascended* plane of existence where we are further purified and refined. In the ascended plane of consciousness we are able to transmit the light of God-Power to those on the descending planes of consciousness.

6. Finally we either return to the earth plane in future incarnations in order to work out our destiny or we continue on to a *cosmic* plane of consciousness where the soul returns to the God-Source from whence it came originally.

When we are discussing the development of higher mental powers we are also skirting close to our divine power. Thus, to a certain extent, what we are undertaking is a quest for our spiritual selves. When we locate our soul-self and understand how it operates in the cosmos we are able to demonstrate such attributes as harmony and healing, clairvoyant understanding, prosperity and success, love and intuition, originality and creativity.

Awareness—the miracle key

The miracle key to these higher mental realms is increased awareness of them.

We actually have several levels of awareness operating simultaneously. The purpose of psychic awareness and cosmic attunement *is to create clear channels* to the deepest levels of our awareness. Roughly speaking, our conscious level is ruled by senses, words, and reason. The subconscious stores our memory and past experience. The superconscious level is the seat of our extrasensory knowledge. The divineconscious is our own inner contact with divinity.

The doors to psychic awareness

Since you contain a portion of divinity within you, you are capable of being an instrument of the cosmos because you are related to everything else that has been created by the cosmos. The same cause that created you also created everything else! The magic door to psychic awareness is opened when we still the conscious demands of our minds and bodies and look within to the deeper levels of awareness.

The most ancient method, and still the most effective, is meditation. For many students of the occult, meditation is the *only* method for reaching the spiritual selfhood within.

Your interior self may be quite different from your exterior self; nevertheless, it is a portion of your mind which is active in your life.

BRENDA'S PROBLEM OF FRIENDSHIP

"I only have one problem but I think it is a big one," Brenda began our interview.

"What is that?" I asked.

"Well, to put it frankly, I have trouble making and keeping friends. I no sooner get acquainted with someone new than I seem to be on the outs with her or him," she answered.

"Why are you seeing me?" I asked.

"Because I'm beginning to think it may be me instead of them," she laughed.

As we probed deeper together we found that Brenda, a married woman in her forties, had a problem that was even more basic than the one she was describing. There was no legitimate reason for her to be without friends or to have her friendships disrupted with arguments or distrust. She was a cheerful, pleasant person who meant well. She had a serene family life and was active in church work. Still, she felt the problem keenly. As it turned out she was not being unfriendly. She simply was "reading" things inaccurately. She was misinterpreting what people said and did. She had a negative orientation which prompted an inability to read the true from the false. A friend of hers could make a statement and Brenda in her sensitivity would view it as a criticism or a sign that the basic trust of the relationship was being undercut. Actually she was over-interpreting.

"When you expect that someone is being critical you actually bring the criticism into play by your own reactions to the situation. You are overly sensitive and you are probably over-reacting. It is possible for you to get a sounder grasp on the reality of these relationships by increasing your psychic awareness and by proving to yourself that you are an instrument of the cosmos. You can be a conductor of good, of harmony, and have relationships that bear fruitage. Would you like to try the techniques of cosmic attunement?" I concluded.

"Yes," she said simply. "I understand your basic technique is meditation."

"Yes," I said. "We recommend a fundamental meditational technique. We'll teach you variations of that method for a variety of purposes. That way you can adapt your meditational practice to suit your needs at the time. It really isn't as difficult or unusual as it seems and everyone benefits from its employment."

We started Brenda on the basic technique of meditation. Within a few short weeks she was gaining a more confident picture of herself, her abilities, and her true place in the scheme of this world. She began to see her own uniqueness, her contribution, and she grew more steady because of it. The former nervousness disappeared, she was able to take life as it came, and her relationships with others became free of turmoil and permanently harmonious. By the end of the second month her family and friends began to remark upon the change in her.

"I guess I made it," she said to me over the phone. "My husband says I'm more beautiful than I was when he first met me."

AN EXECUTIVE'S CONFUSIONS CORRECTED

Lance C., a well-known and highly respected business executive, had a similar problem except that it was work related. As a result of a series of rapid promotions he had a staff reporting to him and several hundred people in his department. However, he was not prepared for the conflicting reports he was getting from his supervisors. He didn't know whom to trust and he was concerned that his reports to his superiors did not contain accurate reflections of what was happening. He needed a better way to receive data and assess it in order to distil the truth. Meditation for increased awareness was the answer. It calmed his thinking and made it possible for him to meet emergencies with ease. He found that he could get at the root of things without running down a blind alley. He found that his supervisors were not trying to deceive him. Meditation provided the key to his ultimate success as a high-level executive. He is an ardent advocate of its benefits.

A BUSINESS BROKER'S DILEMMA SOLVED

Felix R. earned his living by buying and selling small businesses. As a broker of small businesses, he tried to match a seller with an appropriate purchaser. It was for him a way of life that had many annoyances and frustrations. Yet, he was sustained by the thought that someday he would find a business that he himself would buy and successfully operate. It was his secret desire.

Felix had his dream come true as a result of increasing his psychic sensitivity through simple meditation practiced constantly and earnestly each day. He found that he was able to begin foretelling the probable success of the businesses that came his way. He could sense the values, shortcomings, and possibilities of small businesses with only a small amount of information. This meant that he could more exactly fix a fair price for the businesses he handled because his assessment of their potentialities was in keeping with their ultimate performance. In fact, he became so uncanny at it that he refused to handle any business he felt might not be profitable for prospective buyers. His reputation grew steadily.

Finally, he came across a small manufacturing business which seemed so "right" that he invested his savings and purchased it outright himself. His dream came true and today he is the sole owner of a thriving small-parts company. His own greater attunement keyed his higher mental powers into the proper channels to make the buy; and these same mental faculties continue to guide his decisions and actions.

The rewards of meditation

A sense of impending danger can be detected by students of meditation. Many profess the ability to tell when a dangerous situation will arise and can thus avoid placing themselves in its way.

Decisions in general seem to be easier, more certain, for those who meditate regularly.

Basic meditational methods

Almost all meditational methods are founded on simple underlying principles. Meditation is a mental discipline which opens awareness and improves accurate perception. It can be practiced by anyone regardless of intelligence or station in life.

Stated in its simplest form here is a basic meditation outline for beginning the practice of effective meditation:

1. Seat yourself in a quiet room free from distractions and interruptions.
2. Provide yourself with subdued lighting, good ventilation and a comfortable temperature.
3. Sit erect but let your muscles relax.

4. Focus your attention inward, casually searching, waiting.
5. Don't force your attention. Let it wander easily.
6. Repel any negative thoughts which you may have.
7. Let your thought dwell on positive thoughts, someone you love, a scene which is restful and soothing, or a future occasion which you are looking forward to.
8. Next, put your mind in neutral. Let your attention become passive, observational in character, receptive.
9. Conclude with a prayer in your own words.

This simple meditation can be performed in as little as twenty minutes. It is designed to increase your inner awareness and it will help you to focus and control your mental, emotional, and psychical energy.

You will be introduced to more advanced meditational techniques in later chapters. But this outline is the groundwork upon which you will build. You will probably notice a harmonious inner peace begin to take hold of you between the tenth and fifteenth time you meditate in this fashion. When you do feel inner peace and calm it is a sign that you will be ready for varied meditations for more specific purposes.

When you are ready to move forward, you will. As long as you are anxious about getting results you will be held back. So relax and let yourself move according to your own inner tide and rhythm.

Now let's look at some variations of this basic meditational formula and see how it can be applied for a variety of purposes.

Harmony and healings

Mildred X. stumbled on a variation of this meditational system which led to her healing a long-standing ailment in her digestive tract. She had been receiving medical attention. The spontaneous remission of the ailment caused her to conclude that it was the application of her own spiritual and mental power which cured her since no change had been made in her medication. She explained it to me this way. "I had been in your meditation class for several months when it came to me. Why not take step #8, the state of passive mind, and introduce into the subconscious the thought of perfect health? I knew if this was to be effective the subconscious direction had to be subtle yet firm. In other words, I had to direct myself to perfect health but not do it in a way which interrupted the passive state. I wasn't going to bless myself or anything of that nature. I was simply going to call on the power of the cosmos to enter and heal, a very simple request or petition."

Mildred began doing this as best she could. It was a twofold task she had set for herself, to remain neutral, and yet to direct healing rays inward. During the second week of this attempt she felt she was finally mastering the dual technique. Another week passed before there was noticeable change. Then another week and she instinctively felt that the illness had been "removed." She discontinued the medication, waited a week, and consulted her physician. He marveled that the former condition had absented itself and he pronounced her cured. The physician said that he wasn't sure what had caused the cure, but he gave thanks along with Mildred that the cure had taken place.

Make no mistake about it, both medical means and spiritual means can be used together in the cure of illnesses. We would not advocate the use of one of these means without the other. If we were not to use medical means, which God has given us, we would be denying the marvelous discoveries that medical science has made. By the same token, non-medical means can be efficacious, too.

Clairvoyant understanding

Clairvoyance is one aspect of extrasensory preception. It is usually defined as the seeing of an event out of its time-space context. That is, clairvoyance is the seeing of something in the mind's eye, as it were, either before it happens or after it has happened. Seeing an event ahead of time is precognition. Seeing an event after it has happened is postcognition.

This same meditational outline can be used to induce clairvoyant seeing.

One member of our study group had a strong desire to see his past. He was under the impression that if he could re-live some events by clairvoyantly bringing them into his mind's eye he would be able to free himself from the emotional memory of these past experiences. As he described this concept to the group it sounded reasonable enough.

He had always been afraid of people and rarely spoke unless something was really on his mind. An average man in his thirties, he had an assembly-line job where communication with people was at a minimum.

"I'd like to enter into life more," he explained. "My wife says that all I have to do is talk and be more friendly. I think there is more to it than that. I've tried just talking more but it seems like a silly thing to do. Anyway, I feel silly doing it. Maybe it is something in my past."

We decided to ask another group member to help him monitor his mental activity in this project.

The student followed the meditational outline above but did so lying down. When he reached step #8 he simply said "ready."

The monitor then suggested a previous age such as "twenty-two." The student was to immediately state what came to his mind's eye, to share the vision or impression that he got.

To vary the procedure, the monitor would sometimes call out a day of the week or a month in the year such as "Tuesday," or "March." The student was instructed to recall whatever associations came to him when he heard the word.

The study group consumed several sessions with this exercise before a breakthrough occurred. Finally, the monitor said "three"—meaning three years of age. The student began to describe a punishment in which his mouth was being washed out with soap for having used naughty language. His recall of the incident was quite vivid and the description of his reaction to the punishment lasted for quite some time.

His description subsided. The student seemed to be "coming out" of it.

It was a significant session, for in the weeks to come his other punishments, the punishments of early childhood, were described. Frequently he was sent to bed without his dinner, or made to stand in a corner for long periods of time without talking. The mouth soaping was a frequent form of punishment even for wrong doings other than speaking naughty words.

He is now able to express himself with ease and a genuine charm. He is making friends as a result, and has been promoted on the job.

This variation can be adapted during your meditation. When you reach step #8 simply direct yourself to review, as you are led, your past so that you can get greater insight into it. Mentally tell yourself that you will profit from this understanding of the past as you conduct yourself in the present.

A healthy understanding of the past, including your mistakes, will help you plan for a happy and rewarding future. Remember to hold your mind in a passive, receptive state, yet direct it *lightly* to review the past.

This same method can be adapted to a survey of the future as well.

How to cast forward in time

Here is how you can use this same meditation system and cast yourself forward in time to help you make the right decision and take the right action.

Follow the steps outlined above. When you reach step #8, the passive-mind step, direct yourself to gently view the future as you think of it in the present. That is, if you have planned an activity for the day after tomorrow, then call this activity to mind. Don't bear down on it. Simply see yourself performing the planned activity. Review it quickly and easily. You will be able to sense a "feeling" about the proposed action. It may seem right or wrong. Or, you may be led to do it differently, in a different place, or with different people, or at a different time. Your higher mental powers are actually helping you to formulate your future experiences in the present so they will be harmonious, right, and true for you. You are tailor-making your future to suit your future needs and wishes.

How a Widow Cast Forward

Matilda R., a retired lady in her early sixties, decided to try casting forward in time. Her husband had passed on several years prior to her attempt at using this casting forward technique. (He had shared her interest in psychic matters.) Matilda was contemplating a trip by car to her daughter's home about fifty miles away in order to spend the Thanksgiving holiday. Her health was good and she was an excellent driver.

She gave her inner mind instructions to cast forward to the time of the trip just a week or so away. As she did so her thought appeared to be clogged for a few seconds. At first she concluded that she was not passive enough and that through mental tension she had activated her conscious thought. But, as she casually examined the clogged "feeling" she realized that she was being given, or shown, a heavy snowfall. Then she saw her husband, in her mind's eye, standing by the side of the road, all bundled up, shaking his head "no." The meaning was obvious. There was going to be a snowfall and her husband was cautioning her not to make the trip.

Matilda wondered if the entire vision was a figment of her imagination. But she knew enough about psychic awareness to know that she somehow had hurled herself forward in time and, for an instant, received a warning not to take the trip as planned. She canceled her plans to travel to her daughter's home. She wasn't too disappointed because her daughter's family would be able to visit her at Christmas. The amazing part of the story was that a heavy snowfall, a record breaker, did fall on the day she had intended to travel. And it started to fall at a time when Matilda would have been only little more than halfway to her destination.

This incident is not uncommon for those who develop their latent psychic talent; they can cast forward in time in order to get direction.

FIRED FROM HIS JOB—GOT A BETTER ONE

Probably no other experience is more deflating for a man than that of being fired from a job. The self-doubt that ensues while another position is sought is enough to test any man's mettle.

Such was the case with Nick. He came to see me to get advice on where to look for work since he couldn't afford to be without a paycheck for very long.

Nick was willing to try casting his consciousness forward in time during meditation. In his vision he saw a long building which he recognized as a headquarters office for a local chemical firm. He interpreted this to mean that he should go to this firm and apply for a job. He did so the next day and was hired on the spot.

Nick might never have thought of this chemical company on his own since it was a small, independent concern. It would not have been *logical* to apply there. But, by using the higher faculties of his own mind, he was led in the right direction and things clicked perfectly for a better job than he had before!

How to assure prosperity and business success

Henrietta was the regional manager of a direct-selling cosmetic company that employed women to sell in the home. She won the national regional sales managers award three years in a row.

Because of her success the area that Henrietta managed was sliced in half. She had to start from scratch again with half the area and half the number of sales personnel.

She set a goal for herself of three years to build her business volume back to its former level. She was skeptical about her ability to reach the goal. It wasn't that she lacked confidence in her ability to organize and motivate people. She had the obstacles of a smaller population and a less active group of sales representatives. She had been given the less attractive half of the territory.

Henrietta had heard of our classes in basic meditation and decided to investigate because, like many others who seek psychic enlightenment, she had a problem. By a quirk of fate she entered the class for the first time when we were teaching meditation for prosperity and business success.

The technique, a variation on the basic meditational method, is as follows:

1. Repel negative thoughts in a relaxed state of mind.
2. Dwell on positive thoughts.
3. Let your mind glide forward in a neutral state.
4. Vividly portray prosperity with all of your imagination and the full force of your mental and psychical energy. Include a mental exploration of all the avenues of prosperity that could be open to you. Include all the ways in which you would like to see prosperity manifested in your life.
5. Then relax and release these thoughts and focus your attention on something entirely different.

By using this variation of the basic meditational method Henrietta was able to set in motion those forces and circumstances that would bring her greater business success in her new challenge. She continued this exercise at home each evening. If there was a section of her area that wasn't doing well she would visualize prosperity in it. In fact she more often meditated for the prosperity of others than for herself.

Henrietta reached her goal not in three years, nor in two, but in a year and a half. She astounded the folks back at her home office. Though hers wasn't the highest volume region, it was one of the top five by the end of the second year. Her "magic" was impelled by thought power released during meditation.

How Jarvis Got Needed Customers

This same method worked wonders for Jarvis M. who owned a steel fabricating business. Jarvis needed orders from customers. But, most customers had large inventories and simply didn't need to buy.

The problem was that Jarvis had sizable stockpiles too and he had to move his steel, or a large portion of it, within ninety days or he would be in serious financial trouble. He knew that it was unlikely that the steel market would change in ninety days' time, but it might be possible for him to find a buyer, or several buyers, that needed steel.

In using the prosperity meditation, Jarvis varied it to include a scanning for potential buyers. He took the entire country, a section at a time, and scanned it as though he were looking at a mental map of the territory. He focused his attention on each area as though he were attracting the probable buyer.

Other than his nightly meditation, Jarvis did nothing extraordinary in looking for customers. His salesmen didn't vary their pattern of calling on customers; his advertising did not increase. Yet, during the ninety days he was able to sell his steel and cut down on the large inventory. He did not make a great deal of money but he was able to show a comfortable profit and maintain his position in the industry. He continued to use psychic awareness so that he would make more accurate decisions and hopefully not overbuy again or get his business into such an untenable position.

How a Manufacturer's Representative Sold More Goods

Eliot, a manufacturer's representative, used the meditational method outlined above in order to know what manufacturers to represent. He wanted to be the representative of the manufacturer with the products most in demand so he could make as much money as possible.

"Do you really think it will work?" he asked me. "It seems so simple it is almost impossible to really think that meditating on prosperity would bring it about. My wife recommended using affirmations for better health and happiness. I always looked upon it as a kind of self-hypnosis, a Pollyanna way of glossing over problems."

I replied, "Affirmations are a form of deep direction to one's own mind. I can tell you that saying affirmations *does* help many people. Who is not torn by doubt and fear occasionally? All human beings are subject to these feelings of uncertainty. *Just think what damage you can do to yourself by affirming your own doubt and fear!* Affirmations are designed to *reverse* negative thought patterns. They work. As to meditation for prosperity, you might first ask yourself if you really want prosperity. Some people have such a low opinion of themselves that they desire failure as a kind of self-inflicted punishment."

"How do I know it will work?" Eliot shot back.

"Only by trying it. Then you can judge for yourself," I answered. "The thing that meditation does, that affirmations sometimes cannot, is to give direction not only to your own mind but to the minds of others, and to inanimate objects as well. When you realize that minds are connected to other minds and that mind has power over matter, then you will see the rationale for this kind of meditation."

Eliot tried the prosperity meditation several times in a practice session before he undertook to do it himself at home. His first reaction was that it helped him to relax. He remained dubious about the final consequences, but decided to give it a "thirty-day trial."

He used every way he could think of to meditate on the demonstration of his own success. He was imaginative about it, too, which helped increase the number of avenues to prosperity open to him.

After thirty days Eliot reported back. "I feel better. I think things are going well. I'm going to keep it up for another thirty days."

So Eliot continued. His success was increasing. Other manufacturer's representatives said that he had an uncanny sense, that he was in a lucky streak that couldn't last. There were even rumors that he had some secret source of advance information. He was an outstanding success!

Eliot had bought the product, prosperity meditation, for his own, personal use.

Love and intuition

Blanche felt she'd made a terrible mistake in selecting a husband. They had been together for a year and found themselves arguing and fighting constantly. It appeared as though each of them was trying to gain control over the other, to dominate the marriage and make the major decisions.

I had Blanche adapt basic meditation to help clear the mistrust and negation, and make way for outflowing love, affection and trust.

Here is the system that she used.

1. Repel negative thoughts in a relaxed state of mind.
2. Dwell on positive thoughts.
3. Let the mind glide inward in a neutral state.
4. While the mind is passive, let love surge up as a fountain.
5. Direct this fountain of love to the person for whom love is desired.

She performed her meditation while her husband was at work during the day. She used the early morning hours shortly after breakfast when she was fresh and had not yet started her day's activity.

Things started to be slowly transformed. There was no suddenness about it, but gradually Blanche found that she could pour out her love more feeely. Her husband reciprocated with each new demonstration of her love and concern for him. Today they are happily married and can certainly be expected to stay that way.

How Cheryl Succeeded in Landing a Husband

Cheryl was eighteen and husband hunting. She had several boyfriends, but one in particular, Mike, was very attractive to her. But he did not seem eligible. He was still "wild" and anything but ready to settle down into the routine of married life. Cheryl knew this and somehow hoped that the maturing process could be hastened. Cheryl applied a "therapeutic loving" variation of basic meditation. Mike did mature and soon proposed marriage.

Here is the method:

1. Repel negative thoughts.
2. Dwell on the positive aspects of the individual to be loved.
3. Place the mind in a neutral state.
4. See the individual in a perfect state of love, able to give love, and able to receive love.
5. See the individual growing in this love, maturing in it, and advancing in its reflection, and in its demonstration. See the effects of this love, the changes, the improvements which it brings.

Nearly everyone can cite cases of the marvelous healing power of love. Love heals and makes life new and wonderful. *Love is not a matter of luck!* It is a *total relatedness* to the world, to everything and to everybody. Love simply changes people and helps to increase their potential for enjoying life and getting the most from every experience that we as human beings have in common with each other. The story of love and its miracle-working power is infinite. It is as wide as history itself and it plays its mysterious part in the destiny of each life. It cannot be overlooked or even given a subordinate position. It is a primary function of life. It is a need that is related to all other needs. We've devoted an entire chapter of this book to love and its practice. For it, too, is a tool in self-understanding —made all the more effective by increased psychic awareness and cosmic attunement. For if God is somewhere, that somewhere may be the *expression* of love itself.

Self-improvement and originality

If you are seeking to improve yourself, then you are really living!

The essence of life is creativity, originality, change and flux. Nothing, not even oneself, remains the same. This is the beauty of existence. As you learn to use your full psychic awareness and move your life into harmony with everything in the cosmos you will experience the exciting change of the cosmos. We are all instruments of the cosmos and have the capacity to demonstrate that instrumentality. Changes that you can make within yourself, in your thinking, and in the way you feel about yourself and life, will reflect themselves outside your life.

The conditions of your environment change also. And you will learn in this book how to influence and change that environment for perfect, satisfying, rewarding living. We are going on a mental journey that will touch on new ways to live, new ways to think, and new ways to respond.

The creativity and originality that you will demonstrate will take hold of the core of your being and prepare your higher faculties of mind for real enjoyment and satisfaction.

In our next chapter you'll learn how to use your latent extrasensory perception. Later, we'll cover sleep and dreams, mediumship, attracting the right opportunities, cosmic illumination, and protection from malicious psychic attack. On our journey together we will be tempted to take interesting side trips. But, we'll stay on course because a *new* you is our final destination. Your awareness and your attunement are the vehicles for reaching this destination.

Points to remember from this chapter

1. We are born with a spiritual component, our soul, which comes to us as a portion of the God-Power of the universe.

2. As life progresses we learn how to experience the operation of the divine power within.

3. When we leave the body our soul continues its progression through other planes of existence and other levels of consciousness as it is purified and refined. Finally, the soul returns to its God-Source.

4. Meditation is the doorway to physic awareness.

5. The basic meditational method is:

    a. Relaxation

    b. Repelling negative thought

    c. Dwelling on positive thought

    d. Placing the mind in a passive, neutral state of receptivity

    e. Releasing the neutrality and resuming normal activity

6. This basic meditational method can be altered for harmony and healing, clairvoyant understanding, casting forward in time, creating prosperity and business success, and increasing love and intuition.

7. Self-improvement and originality make life a new adventure. Psychic awareness and cosmic attunement are the vehicles for transforming your life.

Hubert E. Pearce, a theology student at the Duke University School of Religion, sat in a study cubicle in the library stacks. He paused and then wrote a symbol on his sheet of

How To Be Guided Through Your Extrasensory Impressions

2

paper. He had five symbols to choose from. Dr. J. G. Pratt, a colleague of Dr. J. B. Rhine, was in the psychology laboratory, then located in the physics building on the west campus. Slowly the professor turned over cards, the now famous extrasensory perception cards developed by Dr. Rhine. Each card contained one of the five symbols—a star, wavy lines, a circle, a square, or a plus mark. Pearce was to guess which cards were being turned over by Dr. Pratt. The result was one of the most astounding displays of extrasensory perception ever recorded. The odds against the Pearce-Pratt series were phenomenal in terms of statistical probability. Yet, this series of runs was the real extrasensory perception breakthrough. The authenticity of Pearce's clairvoyance held up under unbiased scientific scrutiny.

Precognition

Next came precognition, the ability to foretell what cards would be turned up *before they were turned up.* Pearce performed as well as he had when he was applying his gift of clairvoyance to the present. It was one thing to collect thousands and thousands of cases of spontaneous extrasensory perception, but quite another to demonstrate it under controlled laboratory conditions and prove it statistically.

There are other, more spectacular examples. Jean Dixon, the Washington seeress, is credited with having predicted the assassination of President John F. Kennedy, the name of his killer, the assassination of Mahatma Gandhi, the death of both Dag Hammarskjöld and Carole Lombard by plane, Marilyn Monroe's suicide, the adoption of communism by China, and the Soviet Sputnik.

There is the fantastic story of entranced Edgar Cayce who was able to diagnose and prescribe for people unknown to him and many, many miles away. His psychic readings are recorded and stored at the Association for Research and Enlightenment at Virginia Beach, Virginia. It is estimated that he gave more than 14,000 readings between 1901 and 1944. Of the readings on file, about 8,000 deal with problems of the mind and body, 2,500 deal with human relations and psychological problems, and about 2,600 or so are miscellaneous and deal with philosophical questions.

Gerard Croiset, the amazing Dutch clairvoyant, is able to find lost people, predict who will occupy a given theater seat, and even heal through his psychic sense.

There is the tested and retested Eileen Garrett of the Parapsychology Foundation, Inc.

Other names filter into the headlines, like Peter Hurkos of Milwaukee, Arthur Ford, and even Jean Dixon's reporter, Ruth Montgomery, who is searching for her own psychic truth. It seems as though everybody is either doing it or watching very intently while others are doing it. Some are incisive and properly critical like Allen Spraggett of the Toronto Star. Some try to teach others, like Harold Sherman.

How to Begin Your ESP Breakthrough

But, no matter what the experience of these other people, you will be convinced of your own extrasensory ability only when you have your first, or maybe second, big psychic breakthrough. Then, and only then, will you truly be convinced that there is something to it after all. And that "something" may just be the most important experience you are likely to have during this life.

Where do you begin? What is extrasensory perception anyway? What is the "Psi" faculty that the ESP people refer to? The definition depends largely on an expert's point of view, but ours is simple. Extrasensory perception is the ability to *know* without empirical data, and without regard to a fixed position in space or time. Extrasensory perception is, if you will, the overcoming of the time-space axis. It is the overcoming of the "now-moment" in time, or space.

Sound too fantastic? Difficult? Impossible? It's none of these. For we have proven, as much as it is possible to prove anything, that it is possible to develop this sixth sense in people who've never experienced it and in people who never thought they had it.

What Is an Impression?

Extrasensory perception begins with the reception of an impression which appears to arise outside ordinary sense data. That means it's got nothing, or very little, to do with what your five physical senses tell you. It is simply something else. Impressions are like hunches, flashes, daydreams. They are vague or distinct. They can be literally true or they can be symbolic. Most people report that impressions are like feelings. Others will actually say that they see and hear in an extrasensory way.

If extrasensory impressions do not come from our conscious faculties or our conscious minds, where do they come from? They must come from a deeper level of consciousness. And, impressions seem to come from several sources. Some of these sources are definitely external to our minds.

WHERE DO EXTRASENSORY IMPRESSIONS COME FROM?

For our own understanding, let's divide the mind into the following categories.

1. *Conscious Mind*—This is the receiving station of the five physical senses. It is your assimilating mind, your reasoning mind, your logical mind, the mind of language and ordinary perception.

2. *Subconscious Mind*—This is your storage house, the originator of phantasy and dreams, and creative imagination. Your subconscious is where you remember everything that has ever happened to you as though it were on a tape recorder ready to be played back on command.

3. *Superconscious Mind*—This is the residence of your extrasensory faculty. This is where your subconscious mind blends into other minds and is connected with events that haven't even taken place. This is where you can go backward or forward in time. This is the part of your mind that can travel about unlimited by your present position in space. It is through this activity of your mind that you get your truest extrasensory impressions.

4. *Divine Mind*—Divine Mind is that spark of Divinity called your soul which is in you and every living thing. It is part of the Greater Divinity which we call the God-Power of the Universe or Infinite Intelligence. It is the causative force behind all people, things, and events.

When you listen for the inner clues, voices of intuition, extrasensory revelations of what you should do, you automatically open your entire being. You judge each experience individually, within its own framework of meaning. Defensiveness and rigidity of interpretation cease.

You are more conscious of reality as it exists, rather than viewing it in preconceived categories. This view actually makes you more realistic in dealing with situations, enables you to evaluate with greater clarity.

Through the complex methods of weighing and balancing your truest feeling, you are able to reach within and locate that which is satisfying and true. It is a growing process, not a stagnant insulation from the world. It is involvement in life; it is your own extrasensory potential being put to use for you.

Some ordinary and not so ordinary case histories of ESP

Mrs. J. S. was in her forties, active in civic affairs, and the wife of a prominent executive. She had three children, all in their teens. She had attended one of our study groups and had learned the basic technique of extrasensory perception. She had made herself aware of her own extrasensory faculty and she could, as a result of her daily practice, tell the difference between a genuine extrasensory impression and a thought which originated in her own subconscious mind. As she sat in her Michigan home one morning drinking coffee, something unusual came to her. As she tells it, she was looking out an upstairs window onto her lovely garden below. Suddenly she saw her mother sitting in a rocking chair, eyes closed, quietly rocking back and forth. But—her mother lived in Cincinnati and couldn't be in Michigan and Ohio simultaneously!

Mrs. J. S. concluded, as a result of her training, that two basic explanations could account for this phenomena. One explanation was that her mother was experiencing an astral projection and this was her astral or etheric body in the garden below.

The other explanation was that her mother had passed on and had come to enjoy the garden in materialized form. The vision shortly dissolved; however, a phone call would help clarify the issue.

Calmly, Mrs. J. S. called the Cincinnati number and found that her mother had been admitted to the hospital in a deep coma. They didn't expect her to live and the members of the family were being summoned. Mrs. J. S. made plans to go of course and, as she did, she made a note of the time the vision had appeared in the garden.

When she arrived in Cincinnati she learned that her mother *had already* passed on just *prior* to her phone call. The amazing thing was that the time of her passing was officially listed as 10:12 A.M., the exact time that Mrs. J. S. saw her mother in the garden!

A OUIJA BOARD EXPERIENCE

"Many moons ago I lived. Again I come. Patience Worth my name." So began the eerie encounter with a discarnate person who decided to communicate by means of the Ouija board. Patience came to an average housewife, Mrs. Curran. On a hot July evening Mrs. Curran and a friend, Mrs. Hutchings, were playing at the board when the Patience Worth message came through. Over a period of years Patience communicated with Mrs. Curran in perfectly constructed seventeenth-century English. Two of her novels were actually published as a result of this form of communication.

REAL ESTATE BUSINESS SUCCESS DUE TO ESP

Jeb M. was a successful real estate salesman. He had been commended over and over again for his sales ability and became an important business figure. I knew him long before I developed an interest in psychic matters. He studied hypnosis keenly and was fascinated by human behavior and the higher realms of the mind. One day I asked him his key to success. (His firm had grown into a multi-million dollar brokerage house.)

"First I tell myself that I can do it," he said.

He went on to tell me the story of how he mentally tuned in on people to find out how to motivate them, how to get them to say "yes" to his ideas. First he relaxed and gave himself the direction that he would tune in on a particular person. Then he let his mind be receptive and neutral. He didn't try to force an impression. It was through his intuitive clues that he set his course of action, made the sale, closed the business deal, or whatever his goal happened to be.

How ESP Helped Anna Become a Bride

One of the most amazing cases of extrasensory perception used for an individual's personal welfare was that of Anna M. who worked at a large public utility. She had been the librarian for the company for over fifteen years. She was unmarried and everyone had lost hope that she'd ever "find a man." She had a mild curiosity about psychic things and we had lunch together from time to time. I'd tell her my latest ESP experiences and she was always amused with them.

We happened to have one of our regular lunchtime sessions on the first day of June. I remarked that it was the month for brides and she replied, "Yes, I know. I'm always the bridesmaid, but never the bride." It surprised me to hear her say this because she usually did not refer to her "state of being unmarried."

"Why don't you try your own ESP? Just tell yourself that the husband of your dreams will come along. Then let yourself be led by your own inward knowing. Don't try to be too logical or reasonable about your movements in time or space. Just let yourself be carried by the tide of events and your own instinct for extrasensory action will bring your husband to you."

I tried to give her a three-minute course in extrasensory decision making, the whole point of which was to try not to be conscious of everything all the time. I explained that being too logical is a hindrance, that ESP works best as a vague "feeling" about the rightness or wrongness of a thing, rather than as something that always hits you like a bolt out of the blue.

She tried not to be ruled by her conscious, reasoning mind during the day. She let herself enjoy the luxury of daydreaming at times and took a walk each lunch hour. But, she didn't plan her walk, she just allowed herself to be led in a random fashion. She decided one day, while walking past the Automobile Club offices, to go in and join. And that's where it started. A year later, June to be exact, she was married to a widower, a widower who worked in the Auto Club whom she met when she decided to join.

When I congratulated them at the wedding she replied, "That's ESP."

How to find what you want through ESP

Ever try to find a place to live by using extrasensory perception? One woman in our study group found an apartment building with a vacancy. She had seen it in an impression after she'd asked herself where she should look.

Ever wonder if you could use your extrasensory perception to get a good buy on something? A teen-age boy in our study group got his first automobile by following a hunch while he was looking for the *right* car, at the *right* price. He located a used car lot that had what he wanted by just following his own inner guidance system as he drove.

Ever think it would be fun to use your extrasensory perception to get someone to telephone you? It can happen all the time, even in an emergency. A college student studying unfoldment with us did just that to reach out, through his own mental telepathy, and ask his girl to call him when he was ill and couldn't rouse anyone else who could get him to the school's infirmary.

What are your impressions saying to you?

Extrasensory impressions can come from several sources at once. They can come from your own subconscious mind, they can come from the minds of others through your superconscious mind, or they can appear as revelations directly from the God-Power arising in your Divine Mind.

Impressions can be helpful to you because they can explain the past. Something may have been troubling you. Just what does a past experience mean?

When an Apparent Transfer Really Meant Promotion

Dick R. had been transferred to the New York City office. It was a promotion but only a slight one. He didn't know how to interpret it. The move didn't seem logical to him. He was doing well in Dallas. It looked as though he would become the regional manager there. But, in New York he had an insignificant staff position. In addition, he reported to a man who was difficult to work with. His wife didn't care for the move either because her friends were back home.

Dick wrote to me, telling of his promotion and the negative situation that surrounded it. He asked what he should do. My interpretation was quick in coming for, as I read the letter, the pictures began to form and the impression came through immediately. Dick was being prepared not for the regional manager's job but for the higher position of vice president. The transfer to New York City was a testing time. His past experience had been too closely associated with but one region. He would have been perfectly qualified for the regional job, but the company wanted to know if his capability extended beyond even that excellent position.

I wrote my answer quickly and sent it to him with the advice to relax, dwell on the positive, and *know* that there was a force working for the outcome of total good in his life. He was being watched and evaluated. He was being tested, and to meet the test he must simply have faith that he would do the right thing. That way he would attract all good to himself and people and events would work to his advantage. "Follow your own extrasensory hunches and don't get jammed up with negation," I concluded.

Only six months later he wrote to tell me of his new position, vice president. This time he was transferred to Washington, D.C. He and his family settled in a beautiful suburb in Virginia and they are all very happy. Someday he may even get another promotion.

INSIGHT INTO PRESENT CIRCUMSTANCES

Extrasensory impressions can also give you insight into your present position and circumstances.

Mabel M. was interested in spiritual matters. She was religious, but without any formal training. Her view of psychic matters was open, intelligent, and broad based. She read widely in the field but couldn't seem to find the proper thing to do with her interest and energy. She knew she wanted to help others. But she couldn't find the right vehicle. She had been the editor of a weekly newspaper, she'd been active in politics, and she had a fine husband and two children in college.

Mabel came to see me for a psychic consultation. She was more interested in the meaning of her present state of indecision than in anything else. The extrasensory impression that I received was simple indeed. "This is your regenerating period. You are being renewed, revitalized and filled with new vigor," I said after a few minutes of conversation.

"Within a year you will be doing something new. This something is being made possible by this period of renewal," I continued, "so don't be frustrated by it."

We then went on to other matters. A year later she became interested in a healing prayer group. She formed one of her own and it met each Thursday morning at her home. Many miracles were reported in the group as a result of its efforts. Not only healings, but changed lives and reformed situations resulted. They were spreading love and harmony to all they came in contact with. Mabel had found a fulfilling outlet for her energy and her interest in the psychic and spiritual side of life.

FUTURE TRENDS INDICATED BY ESP

Extrasensory impressions can also indicate the trend of the future and guide you in decision making.

One of the most exciting aspects of ESP is its ability to

foretell the future either as a warning or in order to give us something to look forward to.

"If you knew the future ahead of time what would you do?" she asked. She had made her appointment without giving a name. She was what I call the "ladies and gentlemen of mystery" who don't want you to know who they are but expect you to tell them things about themselves that *they* already know as proof of extrasensory perception. Their behavior is usually predictable. A furtive telephone call—"Are you the man who claims to be psychic? May I see you Saturday at ten o'clock?" It is a set conversation.

This particular woman was nervous and skeptical at our first meeting but managed to get her concern out about the future. "Well, what do you want to know about the future?" I asked.

She answered crisply, "I know my husband is going to die. Within a few months. I dreamed of it even though no one had diagnosed it or told me. He is in perfect health."

"Then, I'd do my best to make these last months especially happy for both of you," I said.

She visited me once more. This time it was a few days after her husband's funeral. He had died of a heart attack, suddenly, at his office. She had tried to make the last few months happy. He had also appeared in a dream to her on the night his body was buried and thanked her for a beautiful life together. Her knowing the future made a difference. She knew that his time was about to come and she carried herself with pride and with loving tenderness.

How to interpret impressions

Sometimes extrasensory impressions are more symbolic than literal. An impression may come in very clearly but its meaning can be obscured by the symbology.

Following are three ways to help you interpret your impressions.

First, the key to the interpretation of a complicated or highly abstract impression is simply the meaning that the particular symbol has for you. For example, a scene by a beautiful lake may mean tranquillity to you. Or, it could mean loneliness and apartness from people. Or, it could mean something basic, natural growth, the seasons, air and water. Ask yourself the question: what does this symbol mean to me usually?

The *second key* to interpreting symbols is to make your mind neutral, a "blank" or receptive. Then re-create the symbol in your mind's eye. It will evoke other symbols from your subconscious mind. Those symbols will cause others to form, and so on, until you've reached a final meaning which is vastly important in its relation to the original symbol. Yet, this final meaning would not have been made known to you unless you allowed yourself to go through the process of finding the final meaning in this step-by-step way.

Third, if you submit the symbol, or series of symbols, to your own subconscious mind just before you go to sleep, you'll be working it out while you sleep. Often, you'll find that you have the meaning just as you awaken the next morning. Sometimes it will come during your meditation period the following day. You are actually allowing your mind the time to follow the symbol along to its final meaning while you sleep. You may even dream about the impression for several nights before it becomes clear to you. But it will be worth waiting for. It may contain a warning, or it may be suggesting a course of action; it may reveal a deep feeling, or it may even be pointing the way to a new phase in your life.

Basic techniques in developing extrasensory perception

Here are two basic techniques for building your extrasensory awareness. They can be used during meditation to help you overcome the time-space axis. With these exercises you can move out of your present location in time or space. *You will encourage impressions to come to you.* You will awaken your psychic centers. Extrasensory impressions will be built even when you are not doing the exercises. These exercises should be performed each day for about six weeks. You will begin to notice improvement right away but by the time the six-week period is up you'll be getting extrasensory guidance even when you least expect it.

SPACE-LINE EXERCISES

Exercise No. 1

a. Relax. Make your mind a blank.
b. Decide where you would like to visit, a destination.
c. Create a pinpoint of light about six inches from your forehead.
d. Feel as though you were that pinpoint of light.
e. Gradually move the light upward, out, into the sky.
f. Then, move the light, in the sky, to the point where it should descend (its destination). While it is moving, see the terrain below as you would see it in flight. Picture the cities, rivers, mountains, and plains.
g. Let the light descend at its destination, allow it to look around, picking up thoughts, feelings, visions, and voices.
h. Return using the same process. Make notes on what you sensed.

Exercise No. 2

a. Relax, make your mind a blank.
b. Let your awareness float where it will.
c. Make notes on what you sense.

TIME-LINE EXERCISES

The time-line exercises are designed to help move your conscious awareness back and forth along the time line without specific reference to the present. Thus, the past, present, and future are as one continuous line, unbroken.

Exercise No. 1

a. Make your mind a blank while you are in a restful, quiet, relaxed, and passive state.

b. Select a person or place.

c. Re-create that person or place in your mind's eye.

d. Allow a setting to create itself around that person or thing.

e. Describe that setting, or write it in your diary.

f. Re-create the original person, place, or thing, Then, move it backward in time.

g. Describe the backward setting and make a note of it in your diary.

Exercise No. 2

a. Make your mind a blank while you are in a restful, quiet, relaxed, passive state.

b. Allow a picture of someone to form in your mind's eye. Do not select a person, simply allow someone to come into thought.

c. Allow a setting to form, let it dissolve, and permit another setting to form, let it dissolve, etc.

d. Make notes of the various settings, the actions performed, and of the feelings you had.

How extrasensory perception works

The earliest and still most common example of extrasensory perception is the forecasting of events in dreams. The Old Testament is full of such dream sequences in the Torah or ancient Pentateuch. Dreams are the very first things many psychiatrists investigate for a good look into our unexplored "other selves."

Consciousness is the world we see with our five senses; it is the world we know about, the one we live in, the one where day-to-day action is born. It is the place where things *happen*. But "beneath" the conscious is the area we are not aware of. Here we store the detail of our lives. Here is where we remember everything that ever happened to us, even though sometimes that memory escapes our conscious mind. Often hypnotists are able to reactivate the forgotten detail enabling us to recall, often with great significance, the earliest days of our childhood.

It is herein that most extrasensory perception probably takes place. It is where our dreams originate. It is where our innermost desires are born, and live, and rule our lives, from behind a wall, as it were.

Before psychiatry was developed, hypnosis, or induced sleep, was used to tap the hidden mind of the subconscious. But it had been suggested by wise men long before the time of Freud, the father of psychiatry, that our subconscious mind might be related to other minds. Professor Jung used the words "collective unconscious" to explain our ability to share our lives with all of humanity through a mechanism that we all share in common, deep within our minds.

To a certain extent we all have the ability to use extrasensory perception, because we all share the collective superconscious explained by Jung.

The six-fold daily plan

How Extrasensory Perception
May Change Your Way of Life

New perception, like new knowledge, can change your way of life. To what extent, and in what way, is up to you. My hope is that what follows will help change your life in some beneficial ways. Possibly you'll be an excellent psychic automatic writer, or a good person with an accurate "hunch" now and then. In any case, enjoy your new found powers, rule them, don't let them rule you.

For many people, just embarking on the Six-Fold Daily Plan is enough to generate other kinds of self-discipline. Some have written to me that as a result of a few simple consultations their life has gained meaning through new found interests, avid reading, going to lectures on particularly interesting subjects, starting an effective and well-rounded diet for better health, and still other ways.

Some of my clients from the world of show business attest to their newly found ability to make more accurate judgments of new productions.

Let there be no mistake about it, the following six steps are simple. They are designed to develop as much perception of the world, and of yourself, as possible. But their success depends not only on your own innate talents but on your earnest, habitual repetition of the steps in the whole program.

How to Begin the Six-Fold Daily Plan of Extrasensory Perception

First, keep a goal in mind. Your purpose is to maintain a well-balanced mind, one where you can control the various impulses coming from the subconscious, the powers arising from extrasensory perception, and at the same time participate in the world of conscious reality. You must eat, sleep, work, and love, and be very much a part of the normal healthy activities around you.

Next, you begin the Six-Fold Plan of Extrasensory Perception Exercises. These may all be done during a normal day and, in fact, work best when we incorporate the entire program into a fixed routine. For most people I recommend modest beginnings, increasing the complexity of the exercises gradually.

Confusion, unhealthy thoughts, and weak vacillation melt to be replaced by healthy and loving knowledge of the inner self, the world at large, and those you love and care for. It is like an electrical charge, touching all those who know you, and comes from the very depths of your mind. Following are the basic steps for your organized program.

1. *The Waking and Breakfast Period*

Dreams are with you at this time, and they are crucial windows on your psychic presence. A tablet beside the bed to record whatever fragments of thought patterns are freshest in your minds when you awaken starts the day. Then the tablet should be put aside for use later during the meditation period, for subconscious fragments will reorganize themselves fully as the new pattern of self-unfoldment, truth, and understanding frees your creative nature.

While going about your normal morning's routine, we recommend no conversation or interruption by radio or TV. This should be a sanctified time.

A. This is the time of day when your senses are at their best, and it is a good thing to get them gradually alerted to the work you will put them to later on. Sharpen them by clearing each one in turn: sight, hearing, smell, feel, taste, and so on. Tell yourself, "I hear exceptionally well today." Listen to sounds you might otherwise ignore. Make sure you hear everything. Listen carefully. Do this with each of the other senses in their turn.

B. Begin the blending process, that is, blend the senses. Try to literally hear with eyes, see with your sense of feel, and so forth. Bringing your imagination into play you thus help to unclog the inspirations that will arise from the collective natures of the superconscious. You are helping the roadways to establish themselves by attributing to each fundamental perceptor, or sense, the qualities of each of the others.

C. Finally, you are ready to stretch your hidden powers to their fullest. Recall specific sounds, imagine particular sights, imagine a certain touch from the previous day. Recall older sights and sounds, then alter them, rearrange them in your mind to fit your new mood. Recall disharmonious experiences, put yourself in a new relationship with them, then erase that particular set of disharmonious experiences and bring in another. You are actually bringing the clearing process into action by recall. The ability to recall, to feel the former situation with detail, as if it were happening in the present, is a vital step in overcoming the fixed time-space conclusions we have been falsely taught. It enables you to re-evaluate the disharmonious experiences in light of new truth about them.

D. Next you are ready for projection. On the basis of recall you will be able to project yourself into future action, happenings, states of mind, for yourself and others, in such a way that you will be able to organize and project success yet to come by bringing it to your psychic mind ahead of time.

Some call this process "prayerising,"—and to a certain extent it is. But when psychic presence is our guide, then prayer technique is only a single aspect of our projection of the future success.

E. Close this exercise by recording the morning's experiences in your diary. Abstract shorthand (essence of thoughts), not complete sentences, is best for your diary. By writing your insights this way you help organize their deepest meaning for use in meditation, later in the day.

2. *The Working Day*

Intuitive perception is the neighbor of clairvoyance. Psychic occurrences draw on spirit guides, the protective angels, who are working with us for the great unfoldment. But first-level intuition is accomplished almost naturally, without outside assistance.

On your way to work, and throughout your routine day, you will notice that certain people, casual people you pass, bring important insights to your mind. You can't help getting impressions of them, their state of mind, their background, their destination, their jobs, their ages; insights about them are evident. The power to decipher the condition under the surface of things is a vital first step to psychic knowledge and awareness.

During the waking day, during your meetings with people, effort should be made to encourage these impulses, to see them, to know them, to work with them, to understand what motivates people underneath. You will gain mastery over situations, experience that is the basis of leadership of all kinds. *Every successful politician, businessman, every leader of men has developed this power of insight.* They develop it, utilize it for mastery over people. They want to lead, and they gain *psychic insight* of what moves people subliminally (underneath the surface). It is a power of the first level and one that almost every serious student has to a surprising degree.

Gradually, you may be able to try automatic writing or sending or receiving telepathic thoughts from others in need and projecting to them new energy, love, power and greatness, psychic gifts, and personal truth.

There may be some days when you are "dry," that is, when ESP seems very difficult. At other times, it will be easy. That is to be expected. The idea is to develop the habit of using ESP so that you can use it as a preparation for advanced power. Conclude every day with a harsh spiritual stocktaking and set a self-improvement resolution for the next day. Make sure not to be too sweeping with resolutions; they should be easily performed, and for the next day only.

3. *Entering the Sleeping State*

You should always be ready for sleep and pleasant dreams.

The best sleep is complete, deep sleep, that allows full mind and body rest. Partial sleep or light sleep which permits some of our conscious faculties to be responsive to the slightest noise is not deep, recuperative sleep. The conscious mind must recede and the five senses lie dormant. Sleep is an art, defining inner well-being and psychic unfoldment. The simple process of undressing before retiring can be put to advantageous use by banishing all worrisome thoughts and the high-pitched activity of the day from your mind. One should not proceed to sleep until all discordant thoughts have been abandoned and put to rest in the subconscious mind; otherwise a restless and unbeneficial sleep will result.

4. *Exercise*

Proper diet and exercise are imperative in good psychic conditioning. Regular exercise in keeping with your age and health is essential. The exercise should be strenuous enough to absorb your mental activities. It is the only way we have of diverting our concentration from psychic activity long enough for a natural equilibrium to take place.

This equilibrium between psychic presence and workaday conscious activity gives our psychic insight an opportunity to catch up, to integrate new experience, new psychic gifts. We are very much a part of the world, that is why we are gifted in the first instance. That is also why we cannot remove ourselves completely from the world, why exercise brings us back to conscious reality.

5. Prayer Life

Your whole life can be summarized as a prayer, or thanksgiving. As you walk in cosmic attunement, you'll realize that you are praying always. Prayer is a natural response to the excitement of life and its wonderful experiences.

The last thoughts before sleep should be ones of rest. Put your entire well-being in the faithful trust of Infinite Intelligence and Godly protection. Visualize your very being, your very essence, as it may be lifted to God in rest. Prayer, thoughts for others, wishes, desires, blessings, should occupy your mind as you visualize the great quiet waters of truth and healthfulness reaching down and touching your soul.

6. Finally, Comes Your Meditation Period

This is the peak of the productive day and should occur just before sleep. It is best to pick a restful, quiet place and a specific time each day. Your dream note pad from the morning and projection diary provide the basic material for the contemplation period, at least as a starter. Then you develop a series of questions you hope to have answers to by the time you wake the next morning. Include any distorted signals you may have gotten from people during the working day, and try to sum up by setting a resolution for yourself.

Do not, at any time, "fight" with yourself or your abilities. Don't try to mix a helter-skelter, rush-around existence with psychic development. It simply won't work. To do so is to ruin your health. You are to allow mystical experience to take place. You can't, then, force it upon yourself. Knowledge, in a sense, happens to you. Enjoy yourself, let worry depart, especially during meditation. Relax all over, and your state of mind will improve right away. Your powers take a little time.

Your ESP meditation outline

The meditation program should be organized each day, the general structure should be the same, although the material will vary, of course. Let the following plan work for you:

1. SILENCE

It is a good idea to begin with just a few moments of silence. This should help relax the senses and call the psychic *presence* into action. Feel your mind going backwards into the inner recesses, the psychic presence depths, across the planes of existence. A quiet, darkened place, regularly available, is best for this important first step.

2. DREAM INTERPRETATION

Next come the fragments or basic patterns from the morning's dream pad; let each of the scenes come back to you effortlessly, remember as much as you can, then recall other similar scenes. Take each word from the recall scene and follow that word backward through free association to its original, personal meaning. *There is almost always an important message from the psychic presence in our dreams, and the dreams need to be decoded by recall before you can project them into future unfoldment.* Remember all significant emotions surrounding the recall words and scenes.

This process frees the mind, so that the Divine Mind insights may vibrate their way freely into your consciousness. In recall, the technique used is to follow one word or scene backward, again and again as it were, until the series of scenes or words concludes. In this way a series of new meanings becomes evident. One scene suggests another, which in turn suggests a third. Finally a basic continuity emerges, which is the clue to the clairvoyant message. You will find the process becomes automatic as you progress with the program.

By following each detail to its final resting place, gradually you put the jigsaw meanings into place and the entire vibration of the reading becomes clear, the decision is made.

It is important not to look for logical responses, the first ideas which come to your mind should be heeded; follow further scenes quickly, *before your conscious mind has an opportunity to intervene.* You will be amazed by the most accurate revelations, the clues to future successes and effective personal decisions.

3. TEXTS

Guidance texts, either from the Bible or from great books, should be next. Read over a few phrases to yourself, then pause and contemplate on their full meaning for your life, and for your loved ones. *It will surprise you how psychic awareness will come to you by doing this.* New prophecy, and possibly even clairvoyant mental healing, will wing its way to you and others in need of your help.

Often a very remote idea, taken from a text, will suddenly bring to the fore an entirely new meaning for your future or someone else's. The underlying patterns are what we are looking for, and the same association process operates with texts, as with dreams, with simple free association, and finally in trance.

For example, if you choose a text about a mountain, and while contemplating you see a friend of yours come into vision, then the conclusion might be that the friend may be about to have a significant experience in connection with a mountain. It may be simply a trip to the mountains, or it may be more complicated; the mountain may stand for something else, a roadblock in that person's life, or it may mean some special kind of love or financial development. Through further investigation of the meaning of this combination of signals, through recall, association, mental wandering, the ultimate message stands out. The principle here is that the insignificant or irrelevant, when followed by their natural conclusions, have the most profound implications for the future.

The example above is a simple one of course, but it should be remembered that one meaning, or insight, placed next to another, freely arrived at, brings a third meaning, related to the first two, but with a final psychic meaning of its own.

4. FREE-ASSOCIATION PERIOD

Next, let your mind simply take its own direction by itself. Try to think freely of "nothing at all." It is impossible to think of nothing, and when we *try* to do it, our mind quickly fills with a series of unrelated images—often even more scrambled than the ones arising from the text meditation or dream interpretation. But, whatever does come to your mind, you should *write it down* for use later, just before you go to sleep.

This free-association period, as I call it, gets the deep psychic energy going. When we try to think of nothing, we are close to the trance state. Our conscious mind takes a leave of absence to a certain extent, and the subconscious walks forward with the impulses from the psychic presence. These images are important. They are fresh, often brand new. And they need to be committed to subconscious work during sleep, so they may reappear as dream material the following morning.

5. PRAYERS

Conclude your meditation with a few prayers, a general stocktaking, and a resolution for the next day.

Later when you go to sleep, let your mind drift over the items you wrote down during the free-association period. Ask that you may know about those items before you wake, possibly in dreams.

The material from the meditation period enters your subconscious for dynamic action during sleep; you regain the same psychic presence material, revitalized as dream material, the next morning. You will write it on your dream note pad and utilize it in that day's meditation period. Unfoldment will come startlingly alive for psychic awareness works by the slightest suggestion.

How does your psychic awareness participate in this important process? Your prayer period and your meditation period formulate questions and answers coming from your psychic presence. They will be somewhat tentative at first, since you cannot command action. But they will bring about ultimate harmony, peace, health, and success. You must continue these exercises in an intense and positive manner. You must visualize Divine Mind coming to life, within you; see it taking shape; feel your mind freeing itself; feel your life changing. As you proceed step-by-step, you will find divine inspiration, the psychic presence, working to harmonize all your feelings and actions.

Personal satisfaction and sensitive unity of all your mind processes will begin to take hold of your very destiny.

All mind forces near you, operating on the same vibratory pattern of psychic presence unfoldment, will aid you in driving out all evil and disharmony. You will be able to summon prophecy and wisdom and mental healing for yourself and loved ones. Your integration and full mind potential is near and you'll be able to feel it come about as new vigor, satisfaction, lust for living.

6. GROUP MEDITATIONS

If you are seeking unfoldment with others, you can perform group exercises, preparing meditations together. In these instances, members of the group, each in turn, state items from the dream pad, and the group analyzes the information. The members let their minds glide inward for the telepathic signals of insight.

The same is done with texts and spontaneous prayers. The group advances together.

Care should be taken in organizing the items to be used, the persons to be called upon, in advance, so that once the group meditation begins, it can proceed under its own momentum without a leader indicating which way it should go. The principle to follow is *spontaneous experience*. Discussion should follow the psychic events, not interrupt them.

Direction from the group leader should be kept to an absolute minimum. The general course of the meditation can be agreed upon ahead of time, so that the momentum is inwardly creative, healthy.

Almost all groups leave time for testimony from members of what has happened in their lives since the last meeting.

Starting and ending a group meeting with silence is essential. Members should not converse either before or after a session, but rather start and end on time and follow the outline proposed. Social occasions are best scheduled separately from study meetings.

Points to remember from this chapter

1. The superconscious mind can receive and send extrasensory impressions. Impressions are like hunches, flashes, daydreams. They can be felt, seen, or heard. They can be literal or symbolic.

2. Impressions come from several sources, sometimes all at once. They can come from within, they can come from other living people, from discarnates, and from God.

3. Impressions are meaningful because they explain the past, give us insight into our present condition, or indicate the trend of the future. They offer courses of action and guide us in decision making.

4. It is also possible to send impressions to other people. Thoughts are things which become experiences for those to whom we are sending them.

5. There is no limit to thought power and the effectiveness of its directed energy.

6. Time-line and space-line exercises can help you overcome the time-space axis and your limitation in the "now moment."

7. The Six-Fold Daily Plan for developing greater extrasensory perception includes the waking and breakfast period, the working day, the sleeping state, exercise, prayer and meditation.

8. Your ESP meditation outline, for use each day, includes silence, dream interpretation, texts, a free-association period, and prayer.

9. Psychic energy can be pooled and insight gained by following the ESP outline in a meditation group.

Joe was driving his truck to Toledo. Just outside the city he stopped at a place where he planned to get a good, solid breakfast. His usual run was Chicago-Detriot. Occasionally

3

How To Attract the Right People and Things for Your Benefit

he drove from Chicago to Pittsburgh or Philadelphia. Toledo was a little off the beaten track for him.

Joe was a widower at the age of thirty-two. He had two young boys aged five and seven. His mother was helping to raise them. His wife had died of cancer and Joe had taken up the study of psychic forces. He was in one of our Detroit study groups and had shown his ability to help others with his gifts for healing through laying-on-the-hands. He was gradually reaching inward and he was finding the higher powers of his own mind—led by intuition. He was at peace with himself even during the long, lonely hours on the road.

As he pulled into the restaurant outside Toledo he felt the "rightness" of the stop. He smiled a broad, Irish smile at a little dark-haired girl who took his order for scrambled eggs, ham, toast, and coffee. "What's your name?" he grinned.

"I'll tell you who I am if you tell me who you are," she answered.

The small talk went from there. There weren't many people in the place, and they talked for quite a while. He asked her if she'd go out with him. She said she would if he'd call later in the week and set a time. When Joe got back to Detroit he did call her. Later, they were married.

Joe gives the credit for finding his new wife to cosmic attunement. He had set his need for a wife into motion during meditation and he was led to the right person. He says he'd never have stopped at the restaurant under ordinary circumstances. But he was alert to his own inner reactions and his extrasensory perception had told him that it was absolutely right for him to stop there.

How a Retired Schoolteacher Found Happiness

Wilma was a retired schoolteacher. She had taught Latin and English in high school nearly all her life. Her only major outside interest was participation in a small church choir. She needed more to do and she knew it. If she were to stay young she would have to find several projects to occupy her time. Wilma tutored students, she traveled a little, gardened.

But she needed a larger project, something that would give her more responsibility. She hit on *the idea* at a study group meeting. She'd like to be a choir director. She had the musical qualifications and played the organ beautifully. Wilma had substituted many times for the choir director in her own church. But who would want a retired schoolteacher as a choir director? She knew that cosmic attunement and awareness would help her locate what she needed. Wilma had supreme faith that sooner or later her problem would be resolved to her satisfaction.

Her chance came unexpectedly. The young people of her church decided to produce Gilbert and Sullivan's *Mikado*. They needed a director with musical training and decided to draft Wilma into the job. She was elated for the entire two months of rehearsals. The performance was a hit.

The young people immediately planned to do another Gilbert and Sullivan operetta. Under Wilma's direction, it was a bigger hit than the first.

In all they produced three shows during one winter! It kept Wilma hopping but she couldn't have been happier. She had attracted the very circumstances she wanted. Each winter Wilma produces three shows with the young people. Every season has been enthusiastically accepted. It's a permanent project and a big one.

How a failing contractor was revitalized

Edward G., aged forty-eight, was a general contractor. His career had had its ups and downs. He had earned, and lost, several fortunes in his life. People said he was in a slump; the creditors were knocking. He introduced himself to me after a lecture on Complete Cosmic Illumination. "I've tried everything else," he said. "I guess these exercises won't hurt. I hope my wife doesn't think I've gone off my trolley."

"Maybe she'd like to try it too," I said. He persuaded her to try. Both of them made arrangements to have three private instructional sessions with me to get themselves going "on the right track." They progressed well during the instructions and we decided that they'd report back every week or so just to make sure they were doing everything correctly. During the third month Ed had something startling to report.

"We want you to know that I've just landed the biggest contract I've ever bid on. It is for a high-rise apartment house in the downtown section. This one not only will get me out of a big financial hole but it will earn a great deal of profit for me. And it'll give me a chance to bid on some other large buildings, too. I'm going to bid on a new shopping center."

He not only made money on the apartment house, but also bid on the shopping center and won the contract for it, too! He's been successful ever since. Ed attributes this good fortune to his attunement with the unseen cosmic forces and continues to study psychic matters as an aid to his business judgment.

Psychic awareness has literally earned thousands upon thousands of extra dollars.

The secret power at work in these case histories

What do these cases prove? They suggest a power of attraction more subtle and far reaching than any which man has discovered in the material world. They tell us that man has the power within his own consciousness to reach out and bring to himself the people, opportunities, and situations which he needs. Our total self extends far beyond the physical. We are also mental, emotional, spiritual, and psychical beings. Psychic awareness brings all this power to you if you will but recognize it.

How to get guidance and direction from the superconscious

The first step in gaining guidance and direction from your superconscious mind—where the past, present, and future exist as a continuous line—is to still the activity of the conscious mind.

Your conscious mind deals with each moment in present time. It is geared to the data that your five sensory mechanisms (sight, hearing, touch, smell, taste) give it. It is the concluding mind, the reasoning mind, the doubting, questioning mind. It reaches its conclusions, decides to take actions, on the data it gets from your physical senses.

CHANNELING THE SUPERCONSCIOUS MIND

In order to overcome the demands which your conscious mind is making, it is necessary to still it. Then you've begun to open the channel to your superconscious mind where impressions are flowing without the hindrances of the sensory world or the needs of logical deduction and reason.

For example, you may be wrestling with a problem, trying to find an adequate solution. Somehow, the more attention your conscious mind gives the problem, the more difficult it becomes. The solution just doesn't seem to be there. Then, exasperated beyond endurance, you give up for the moment, and turn to something else. The minute you let yourself place your attention on something else, and release the problem from consciousness, the solution hits you "out of the blue," as it were. Previously, your attention to the problem had blocked the channel to your superconscious mind and your extrasensory faculties could not help you. Then, as you turned to another idea, and let go of the problem, the solution came to you.

This is the principle of recreation. It is a turning of attention from your *usual* concerns to something unimportant, even possibly frivolous. In doing so, you renew your ability to handle the everyday problems and find solutions.

How to gain release and give your superconscious a chance

When you release a problem from conscious attention you give your superconscious the opportunity it has been waiting for. Your superconscious attracts the people, places, and things that you need to solve the problem. You can actually turn a problem over to your superconscious and forget about it!

Once you've released, all you need to do is relax and wait for developments to take place.

Of course you need to be careful not to let any fear or anxiety disturb the mental vibrations that you've set in motion. The greater reaches of your mind, its cosmic consciousness, synchronizes the people, places, and conditions, in just the correct order and sequence to materialize what you need. By releasing the problem, you set the forces at work for you.

How the Right Real Estate Was Found

Christopher D. was looking for lakefront property on which to build a home. He only had three thousand dollars to spend on the lot. However, most of the suitable lots cost much more, about five thousand. He pondered and fumed, searched and worried. Then he came to me and asked what my psychic advice was. He thought I'd be able to lead him to the exact location he wanted at the price he was willing to pay! I explained that most good psychics could not work quite that way.

We discussed the power of his own mind to bring the solution to him through the right combination of people and circumstances.

He described the kind of lot he was looking for, in detail. Trees, a gentle slope to the water, facing north, with room for a small boat house and dock. The house would be situated about one hundred yards from the water. A quarter-mile road would lead to the location. Utilities would be available.

It was a large order. But, once this description had been detailed, I had Christopher direct himself to release it to his superconscious mind. He let go of it, and spent his time on other, more pressing, matters. It was as simple as that. Two weeks after his consultation with me a man *came to him,* offered a lot, *just like the one that Christopher had visualized,* and at the exact price he'd hoped for. Release? Visualization? It was both!

She Tried Too Hard to Find a Husband

Olga was an airline stewardess who came to me for a private reading. She was only twenty-two years old. Her real interest was finding a husband, the right husband, soon. She didn't want to be "airborne" any longer than necessary. It was clear that locating a husband was her all-consuming desire. It made her tense on dates; she had begun to feel self-conscious about it. "When a friend of mine gets married I feel that I'll never find the right man. I have plenty of boy friends and go out often enough, but nothing seems to click right," she said.

"You are trying too hard," I said. "Besides, marriage naturally follows after love has set in. Why not visualize someone you can love, then release the picture, relax, and let things happen for you? You are probably pushing all the time, and criticizing yourself, and worrying about your actions. Let your superconscious mind do the work," I concluded.

We discussed how to visualize and how to release the visualization. "It's a simple cosmic law that you are setting in motion. It will work if you can release your desire," I said. I wasn't, however, sure she could release this desire.

So, during my nightly meditation I brought her to mind and visualized her in love and becoming the wife of a man who loved her. The extra metaphysical push that I gave coupled with that she was doing did it. She was married within six months. I got an invitation to the wedding, which took place in New York City.

How an Accident Emergency Was Met

Helen made her living by running a boardinghouse for college students near Wayne State University in Detroit. She'd been in the same location for years and had the patience and love that made her an ideal boardinghouse operator. She had been attending our public lectures and had started to practice some of the techniques of cosmic attunement. She located a ring she had lost, visualized her house filled to capacity during the summer (it turned out that way), and she worked on her healing ability.

One morning she was going down the stairs into her basement when she tripped and fell, breaking her right hip. She called, but no one heard her; apparently all the students were at their morning classes. Helen was without a person to help.

She used her powers to visualize help, believing that someone would come to her aid if she released the thought to her superconscious mind. She knew that when she gave expression to the achievement of a difficult objective her mind would be placed on the wave length with other minds that were in a position to respond to the call. As she was releasing her problem, a knock on the outside basement door raised her hopes. It was the man who'd come to read the gas meter.

She called in a loud voice, "Come in, the door is unlocked." The man came in, saw her plight, went upstairs and called an ambulance, and helped the driver put her on the stretcher.

She went to the hospital, was treated for the broken hip, and returned home several weeks later feeling fine again. She had mentally tuned in on the mind of the gas man. He took a different route that morning and came to Helen's house several hours ahead of his usual schedule. Helen asked him what made him take the altered route.

"I just felt that I should. I had a funny feeling it was the thing to do," he said.

How to repel negation

It is just as possible to attract negative thoughts, feelings, and circumstances as it is to attract positive and happy circumstances! You know people who are dominated by feelings of uncertainty, indecision, and confusion. Their minds are never synchronized with the conditions which they find themselves in. They are victims of unrealistic visions and are prey to charlatans and fraudulent psychic practitioners.

Since these people are in a perpetual state of negation, they grasp at the straws of hope, any straws that are randomly offered. In fact they welcome negative conversation and reports of gloom from anyone who'll tell them of failure, disappointment, and fear. They usually don't take any action at all because they are paralyzed with the thought that they'll make another mistake. Life seems to be a risky business at best. It certainly has its opportunities for bitterness and frustration. Nothing goes right for these people. Each failure they have hypnotically brings about another one. Transformation into a positive wave length seems impossible for them, and suffering has become an inevitable way of life.

It is necessary to be careful in dealing with people who are on a negative wave length because they interpret *everything* as further negation. They are looking at the world through distorted glasses, the glasses of their own disjointed, empty lives.

The most effective way to counter a person who starts with one set of negative assumptions and follows it with another and another, is to repel his suggestions right at the outset with a positive thought, action, feeling, or interpretation.

For example, if someone says to you, "What a hot day!" You should counter with, "Yes, it is just what I need to do so and so."

If one of these persons says, "Guess what just happened to me," you know that it is going to be bad news.

Listen briefly, then break in, and start pointing out the advantages and opportunities that the situation presents. Chances are the individual never thought of it that way. Keep pointing out how lucky the person is to have had the experience and show how it is possible to build from that experience into something better and more fulfilling.

One trick of the negative thinker is to call the attention of other people to some impending unspecified danger. They'll criticize something you are about to do, pointing out the pitfalls, exaggerating the risks, trying to immobilize you with fear. The positive response to this tactic is to get at the underlying assumption without hesitation and point out why that assumption is incorrect. If the negative thinker says, "I don't think you should make that investment because you might lose all of your money," your response should be ready.

"In the first place I can only lose what I'm investing and I'm only investing part of my money. In the next place, every indication is that I will make money by this investment. There are no valid reasons to assume it will be a failure." An answer along this line should be ready on the tip of your tongue.

If all else fails, you should quickly terminate a negative conversation. "I have to go now." Or, "I'm expecting another call." Or, "Someone has just arrived. I'll have to talk to you later."

How to look for the positive ways

Positive thought, action, and feeling attract healthy events. Dwelling on the positive brings more and more which is positive. People, situations, and conditions become more positive as you are aware of the positive potential being demonstrated. Following are some tips for finding the positive elements around you so that you can attract even more positive conditions by getting into a positive mental habit. Write the answers out for yourself, and ponder them frequently.

1. What was the best thing that happened to you yesterday? This week? This year?
2. How did these good things come about?
3. If you could choose one positive thing that you could do tomorrow what would it be? (Why not do it?)
4. As you talk with people today, try to find at least one outstanding positive subject to discuss.
5. If you could love people you talk to today, how would you describe that love in each person's case? (Go ahead and think of yourself as loving each person you talk to.)
6. If you could plan for success in your life what would that plan include?
7. What are the positive characteristics of your personality?
8. If you could improve yourself what would you improve?
9. Try *really* greeting the people you meet. Shoot a little cheerful smile, a quick nod of acceptance, and a genuine greeting.
10. When you wake up tomorrow morning think of the beauty in your life.

The positive use of negation

It's possible to build inner strength and security during negative cycles. The best way to handle a series of negative results is to see how they are paving the way for future success and positive happenings. If you've made mistakes and these mistakes have created the negation, recall to your consciousness the mistakes, calmly, one by one. Quietly replace the mental picture of these mistakes with pictures of yourself doing and saying the correct things. Mental correction of past error will develop sound judgment when you are confronted with similar situations in the future. A peaceful mind which has cleared past error generates power and gives you an unobstructed road to those right people, places, and things.

The most energetic man I ever knew, a college football coach, revealed that his secret to overcoming a bad season, or even a losing streak, was to go over the errors the team had made, and correct them. He did this by playing movies of the losing games. The team viewed these films in an effort to detect their own errors and obtain clues to help in correcting them. They did not try to blame each other or find fault. They *replaced* the mistakes with mental pictures of the *correct* actions. They used their poorest plays as food for their own improvement. The team was always alive after one of these film sessions, on fire to win the next game. They never lost their vitality for playing and winning football games.

To them, each game was an exciting event, and they weren't tired or bored.

That's the secret! Get interested in overcoming error. Throw yourself into something with abandon. Lose yourself in what you are doing. Get out of your own lethargy and be a new person. Use every mistake as a stepping-stone to an energy-filled life. Do something now which will overcome the past and make your future one of enjoyment. Mentally, correct the past. Clear it of negation.

How a Marital Triangle Was Squared Away

A man I shall simply refer to as a respected businessman and civic leader was sent to me by his physician.

The businessman, usually considered morally upright, had become involved with a married woman. He was married himself and when he tried to discontinue the affair with the "other woman" she threatened to tell the unknowing spouses and then commit suicide. Naturally this threat gave him pause and the affair continued to become more involved with arguments, reconciliations, and further arguments prompted by jealousy. Since he valued his standing in the community, he was anxious to end the involvement without incident.

When he came to me he was of course ashamed and found it difficult to explain what had been taking place. He slowly managed to fill in the details. They had met at the country club swimming pool and had a few casual drinks together. They enjoyed each other's company. One thing led to another. Here they were, both in their late thirties, both married, both with children.

The more he feared the possibility of being "found out" the less effective he was at conducting his day-to-day business. He had been irritable, picky, and unpleasant to almost everyone and his family was beginning to wonder what was really wrong.

He was processing the most negative thoughts imaginable. He went over every argument, scene by scene, reliving his guilt dozens and dozens of times.

He didn't have time or inclination to start a full psychic development program. But he could make a positive use of the negation that surrounded him. Rather than rethink his mistakes, he was encouraged to replace the negative thoughts with positive forces. He pictured himself saying the right thing, doing the right thing. He visualized an end to the affair that was ruining his life. In this way, he was able to release the situation and confidently await the outcome of good.

Within a month after he had been seeing me—we got together twice a week to review his program—the other woman came to the conclusion that it was "off," and she let him go without a whimper. It seemed that she had "found" another man who suited her better. It gave the businessman just the opportunity he needed, and he terminated the relationship quickly, easily, and without a hitch. Back with his family and wife, he is a happy man. Every now and then he runs into me and usually ends the conversation with, "thanks again for that favor you did for me." He made excellent use of a very negative cycle.

How to create the future ahead of time

Releasing a problem and visualizing the solution are two good ways to bring about change.

Replacing negative thought processes with positive ones can help you avoid a repetition of damaging past experiences.

True happiness and satisfaction can be had by planning the future ahead of time. You do it by becoming *goal oriented.* Rather than spend your time and energy removing discordant conditions, you can work towards a total plan, a goal. Instead of spending your time rushing from one crisis to another, you can carefully chart your future in the present.

Becoming truly goal oriented is the safest, most dynamic way to attract the right people, places, and things in your future.

Goal orientation is a specified set of objectives in life toward which you work.

How to set lasting goals

Goals come to us from several sources, just as thoughts or impressions of any kind do. We formulate goals into words so we can understand them. Goals in their nonverbal form come to us for recognition from:

1. *Conscious Observation*—We observe the goals of others and adopt some of these goals for ourselves. Also, we see that things are not ideal and we would like to make them as nearly perfect as we can, so we set goals.

2. *Subconscious Experience*—Our past conditioning comes into play. We plan future goals and the things we choose to include in our lives, based on our past experience. If something pleases us we decide to include more of it. If another thing brings pain instead of pleasure we eliminate it.

3. *Superconscious Contact*—Goals can be stated in an abstract, generalized way. We are influenced by circumstances which haven't yet taken place, by conditions coming toward us in time. We may not be consciously aware of exactly what the circumstances or events are, but our goal setting, when it is

done with superconscious contact, takes into consideration those things which are not yet evident on the surface.

4. *Divine Presence*—The spark of divinity within is in contact with God's Infinite Plan and helps us to adjust our existence, our own development and progression in this life.

5. *A Combination of the Above*—Any really effective set of goals includes all of the above sources and incorporates automatically the force of cosmic adjustment and greater psychic awareness. That is why once goals are set they often change and undergo refinement as the individual grows and becomes more mature in his mental, emotional, and psychic comprehension of life and in understanding his correct place in it.

There are several things to bear in mind when setting goals that are to last and help attract all good to you—the right people, places, and things. Note the following carefully:

1. Set goals that can rule your *ultimate condition*. Then be ruled by these goals; do not let present circumstances or disappointments hinder your progress.

2. Seek evaluation of your progress. Know where you are *in relation to the goals* which you have set. How far away are you from the goal?

3. Break your goal down into small segments or steps *that you can measure*. Assume personal responsibility for your progress. Don't blame circumstances or other people or things beyond your control. Remember you are learning to control things. They should not control you.

4. Be inventive about your goals, adjust your level of aspiration to that which is feasible and possible. *Don't strive for the impossible*. Be as realistic as you can.

5. *Direct your energy toward the goals*, not toward the frustrations or roadblocks. Initiate actions, don't wait for circumstances to force you to act.

6. Look for goals which offer *alternative courses of action*. Maintain goals which are adaptable to your circumstances and allow you to *keep your energy level up*. Don't choose goals which will tire you.

7. Set goals which will *increase your inner harmony and your serenity*. Goals that can be carried out in an atmosphere of quiet, calm, and confidence are usually the best.

The technique of syndrome creation in the cosmos

Syndrome creation is a technique of manifesting a definite future condition by producing its symptoms in the present. When you demonstrate the pattern of a condition you are making it possible for the full manifestation of it. You are initiating a cause which produces a vivid effect.

How Sandra Brought About a Change She Had in Mind

Sandra was the daughter of a famous attorney. She was enrolled in a private girls' high school and she hated it. "I'd rather go to a public high school because things are normal there. Here it's just one regulation after another," she explained.

"Can you specify what you'd like about a public school and can you tell me how you would be different, how your life would change?" I asked.

Sandra told how she would live at home, her evening hours would be her own, she would have more freedom at school, and most of all she could be herself, expressing her own individuality. Her list of symptoms was long and well thought out. This was not just a whim. She actually considered a public school situation more realistic and a better preparation for life.

I explained syndrome creation to her this way. "You can bring about the change you have in mind. You can make it possible to go to public school by beginning now to express the symptoms or characteristics you'd show if you were enrolled in public high school. You mentioned individuality, freedom to spend your evenings as you choose, and several other differences. The idea is to begin acting now as though you were already in public school. By living now the way you would expect to live later, you are setting in motion a simple cause and effect law known as the law of above and below. The important thing is to list as many of the symptoms, as many of the attitudes as you can think of, that would surround your going to public school. Then begin to live those symptoms. You will be in public school next year if you do this," I concluded. The following year Sandra was in public high school.

The reason? Her parents concluded that she was not the type to conform to life at a private school.

How an Executive Got Out of the Bureaucratic Jungle

John B. was an executive with a large corporation. He had a good job in middle management. But, it often seemed to him a bureaucratic jungle. He was in his late forties and hoped for a promotion. The next rung on the corporate ladder was a big jump. It was the kind of job few would attain to, and those who did usually went on to become vice presidents.

He came to see me reluctantly. He prided himself on his objectivity, on his ability to make the right decisions based on facts. So, seeing a psychic was a little "far out" for him. But he was pleasant and courteous, and listened politely as I spoke.

"You are not acting as if you have the potential to be promoted. The secret is to begin behaving as though you already had the promotion, behave as though you were already in the new job, and you will be noticed by your superiors as someone who has what it takes. Have you ever thought about what you would be like in the new job? Just be like that now. We call this process 'syndrome creation' and it is easy to do. When you leave here today go back to your office and list the characteristics you would display in that higher level job. Then, begin to display them. It is as simple as that."

John left and apparently went back to the office and did as I suggested. He called several days later to say that he was putting syndrome creation into practice. A year later John B. was promoted.

A Marriage "on the Rocks" Saved

An interesting case history of "syndrome creation" was that of a husband and wife who asked for counseling. Their marriage was on the rocks in every way. They were at each other's throat constantly. They didn't want to get a divorce since their church frowned on it but they didn't know how they'd keep the marriage together without really harming each other emotionally or physically.

After several quite difficult sessions during which each one tried to blame the other for the state of affairs, we finally got down to fundamentals, a remedy for the sick marriage. "Has your marriage ever been ideal?" I asked. They admitted it had been about as ideal as anything .ould be for about the first three years. "Do you remember what it was like, how each of you felt during that time?" I had asked the bombshell question. It completely stopped them. I asked them each to take a half hour to describe in writing what it was like. I made coffee for them as they sat with pen and tablet listing what they "felt" during those ideal years.

When they'd finished I explained syndrome creation. They understood what I was saying but I wondered if they'd be able to practice it. I gave them the instruction to go home and behave as though they were in those three ideal years. They were to use what they had written as their guide. "Think and act in terms of the ideal, live it as though it were reality, today," I said. "By acting in this way, by going through the motions that are characteristic of your happy years, you'll start the ball rolling for happiness in your marriage now."

At the next session they said they felt some improvement in the situation. We spent that session visualizing the ideal and releasing the negation and frustration. They were instructed to continue syndrome creation. Within several months, improvement was marked and they were on the way toward a happy marriage.

How to avoid repeating damaging past experiences

Past experiences, particularly negative past experiences, tend to inhibit our growth and understanding. Be on guard against the tendency to repeat past actions in new settings. You can do this by observing your reactions to a negative occurrence in the present and by asking:

- is this negative situation *similar* to any previous ones?
- in what *ways* is it similar?
- how did I *react previously?*
- how can I *react differently* this time?
- what can I do to *prevent this from happening again?*

The answers to these questions will make you alert to the compulsive need to repeat any self-damaging actions. And by being aware of alternative ways of dealing with these situations, you can react differently and change the effect of these experiences.

Love is the magic ingredient

Love is a magic word describing a magical experience. *More is written about love than any other subject!* It is discussed and analyzed, probed and pushed, to the point that it is surprising that anyone still believes in its magical quality. But, the "proof is in the tasting," and the very fact that so many people have experienced it indicates that its value is indeed a transcendental one. The testimony in behalf of love is contained in all major religions of the world and its marvelous effects can be seen at any time and in any life.

Attracting the right people, places, and things is an endeavor that must contain love as its basic ingredient. Love of self, love of a Divinity, and love of others. The difference between manipulating the cosmos, or trying to, and living at harmony with the universe, is love. When love is included in the exercise, or the formula, or the practice, then the psychic result is miraculous. If love is absent the void is obvious to many, not just to the psychic practitioner.

Love is closely related to motive, the reason one wishes to attract all good, the right people, places, and things. When love is the master motive then the cosmic and mental forces that are turned loose are impossible to stop. There is a reconciling, healing, redemptive force at work and its spiritual power does transform lives, it does point people in healthy, renewing, and regenerating directions, and it does affect all those who come in contact with it.

Attracting the right people, places, and things means opening your being to express itself in its fullest human form. Your potential is realized. The thrust of your life is evident. You are in harmony with nature, with the natural, constructive force of the universe through the creative powers of your own mind and your inner self.

Why not give the foregoing a try? The understanding and techniques outlined in this chapter can do for you what they have done for others. They can remake your life, point you in a fulfilling direction, give you new zest, energy, and meaningful experiences.

Life is an adventure which you can share in here and now. The exercises and concepts described are not complicated. You can fit them into your regular routine of daily living. The rest will be up to the cosmic and psychic forces you have set in motion.

Programmed exercises to perform daily:

REPELLING ERRONEOUS THOUGHT

1. Each morning as you arise say the following affirmation for the repelling of erroneous thought patterns:

God is creating perfect harmony in my life. The Power of the universe is rejecting any vicious or malicious thoughts that may be attempting to enter my being. Truth is protecting me and error is evaporating as I concentrate on the divinity within. Erroneous thought cannot penetrate my new understanding of myself, the cosmos, and my place in it. Love is expressing itself in my life and work. Peace, calmness, and harmony are working to the conscious level of my awareness. I am shielded, protected, blessed, and defended by the Power of the universe.

BUILDING HARMONIOUS UNFOLDMENT

2. Each evening before you go to bed say the following affirmation for the building of a positive vibration and harmonious unfoldment within yourself:

I am an instrument of harmony, peace, and love. Every cell and fiber in my body and mind is preparing itself for greater psychic awareness. Time and space contain no limitation as every experience becomes a building block in the unfolding of my cosmic selfhood. I am open and aware of infinite understanding. I am strong and free in God's reflection of truth. My unfoldment is perfection as I attract all good to my vibration and to my life.

VISUALIZATION OF A FUTURE HAPPENING

3. Select a happening that a friend of yours would like to see come about. During your idle moments visualize the event taking place in all of its detail. Ask your friend to do the same. After each visualization be sure to release any roadblocks or frustrations which seem to be blocking the occurrence. Once you have visualized for several of your friends, then begin to visualize for yourself, and your own life, in the same way.

GOAL SETTING

4. Sit down and write out three goals for this week, five for the month, and seven goals for the year. Then, break the goals down into small steps that will lead to their realization. Prepare a chart of these steps and cross out each step as you are able to reach and perform it. Celebrate as you reach each goal. Be sure to reward yourself in some way. The yearly goals call for something extra special. The weekly and monthly goals can be rewarded in a smaller way. After you've succeeded in this exercise prepare goals for your next five to ten years.

SYNDROME CREATION

5. Decide on something you'd like to be. Outline the symptoms and characteristics of that "being." Start to behave in a manner which indicates that you already are that kind of person or being. Use your symptom outline to guide yourself and program your actions and reactions accordingly. Watch to see how soon you really are what you set out to be.

Points to remember from this chapter

1. Negation is any thought, feeling, or action which is destructive to your best interests. Negation can be within and it can come from without. It is necessary to be alert to outside negation and to repel it with positive thought, action, and feeling.

2. Positive thought, action, and feeling attract more creative, fulfilling, meaningful situations, people, events, and opportunities. Dwelling on the positive brings more and more that is positive.

3. By release and visualization you can attract the right people, places, and things. Past experiences tend to inhibit growth and development, especially if these experiences are negative. So, it is wise to be on guard against the tendency to repeat past actions in new settings.

4. By creating the symptoms and characteristics of a thing, in syndrome creation, you can manifest the thing itself.

5. Success is brought about by setting a goal. Then, love is a force which brings the goal into existence.

Cosmic law orders the universe. It is the principle behind that which is seen as *result* in life. Cosmic law is a systematic codification of the truths which are universal. You can use them

4

in your life to yield great benefits.

How Cosmic Law Operates and What It Does for You

How many cosmic laws are there? It is only after trial, error, testing, and observation that they will all become clear to you. Each person has a slightly different understanding of them depending upon his outlook. But they will be evident to you quickly.

You can observe and test the laws we present here. You will be able to reformulate them, restate them, perhaps even add a few which seem valid to you.

The beauty of these laws is that they work without effort. They are unfailing, working in a hidden way which most people are not aware of. The ancient mystics studied their total environment in order to capture the essence of these laws. They watched the stars, observed the regular change of seasons, and came to these same conclusions.

A story has been handed down through the ages that Sarah, the wife of Abraham, discovered this law on an emerald tablet in the cave-tomb of Hermes Trismegistus:

The law of above and below as one

That which is above is like that which is below and that which is below is like that which is above to achieve the wonders of the one thing.

This means that man is the earthly counterpart of God. It also means that God is the heavenly counterpart of man and both man and God use the same Life-Force. This is quite a revelation. God is very much like man. If God is like man, then we can observe ourselves to see what God is. And, if there is One Force used by God and man, then man also is capable of using it. Man is limited only to the *extent* to which he can use it.

This law tells us that man can be like God, or like a god, and can order his life, just as God orders the universe.

We do this by applying the same Force to our surroundings, to ourselves, and to our desires to achieve what we want and need.

How Jim Applied Cosmic Law

Jim, one of our students, was interested in demonstration. We taught him the law of "above and below" and he decided to apply it. He started with his sweetheart. The two were a perfectly matched couple. They'd been going together for several years after having met at a French class at the Y.W.C.A. But, he couldn't get her to say "yes." So, applying the law of "above and below" he kept telling himself that he was ready for marriage and so was she. Moreover, he began visualizing the marriage ceremony during his daily meditation. He'd see it in one setting one day and then he'd visualize it in another way the next day. Finally, Jim began to visualize the marriage itself, the house they'd live in, the kinds of things they'd do. He actually felt moving experiences that they'd have. Christmas with family and friends was one event Jim pictured regularly. Then he visualized the two of them on a vacation together in South America.

Exactly two months after this law was set in motion the couple was united in marriage.

By the time the second Christmas had arrived there was a Jim Junior. They settled in a house just like the one in his visualization.

Jim had invoked this simple law of "above and below." Logic could have dissuaded him from trying this law. But, he gave it an honest try and he demonstrated it in a way which altered the entire course of his life, for the better.

Cosmic laws are more inspirational than rational. You put them to use with your feelings, not by pure reason. You will practice these laws according to the intuitive rightness of your own inner artistry rather than by the outward logic of the law. It is the meaning under the surface that you train yourself to look for. It is the trend of events, the direction of things, which you analyze and understand. Finally, with cosmic law you will be able to change the trend of events. You will start under the surface, at the emotional level, and through your influence of this level you will be able to direct the objective *event*.

Putting cosmic law to work

You will need quiet time to study and observe, to read and reflect. The meditations we outlined in chapter 1 will open your channels to all levels of awareness. Through increased awareness you will be able to sense the true operation of these laws. And once you start along the path, you will reach the goal you have set for yourself.

Every experience is potentially rewarding. What may seem to be random and pointless, is not. Even the apparent mistakes of life have a deeper meaning which is positive and creative. There is a constructive force in everything we encounter.

HOW BARBARA USED PSYCHIC ADVICE TO ORDER HER LIFE

Barbara was shy. She lacked self-confidence. She had asked for a consultation in order to get psychic advice on her life and its trend. She needed some help in organizing what she should do next. She admitted quite frankly to me, right at the beginning, that her main problem was her job. She was a registered nurse in the psychiatric ward of one of Detroit's largest hospitals. She didn't like her work although it paid well. It just didn't give her any job satisfaction. I relaxed and told her what came through to me. I saw rows and rows of books in a library. I described this scene to her. She nodded but didn't show any real sign of recognition of the impression as I described it. I thought that maybe I was getting a distorted picture. Then I noticed a peculiar thing. Every now and then Barbara would be in the picture. But she'd no sooner show herself there than she'd leave and I'd see the rows of books without her.

Suddenly everything went blank. Barbara thanked me and was getting ready to leave.

"It's the Detroit Public Library," I said as the idea finally came to me.

She looked at me still without any sign of expression and left.

Two weeks later, early on a Saturday morning, she called.

Barbara told how she had studied library science before she entered nursing school but had not continued with it. She loved to read. After the consultation with me she went directly to the Detroit Public Library and applied for a job as a librarian. She was hired on the spot at a salary better than the one she had as a nurse. She loves her work and looks years younger.

The Law of Ideal Identification and Mastery

The ideal human being is the one who has experienced and mastered all things.

Many people attempt to hide from life. You may know friends of yours who tell themselves that evil does not exist. They may pretend a disturbing experience was not real. They have insulated themselves from life. But, the ideal state is one of mastery.

The Woman Who Couldn't Get Along with Her Neighbors

A woman came to me for counseling. She was angry with her neighbors. I asked what she was doing to solve the problem. They wouldn't talk to her; she wouldn't talk to them. This had gone on for weeks and weeks. Needless to say, the gossiping was in full swing, too. Neither party had attempted to get together to try to set things straight. The final negative action had just occurred. The lady blurted out, "I got so mad I pulled all my window shades down."

She had avoided the unpleasant. She was insulating herself.

In business situations it is the same way. How often does a businessman delay returning a phone call so he can "figure out" what to say? How often does the salesman call on an easy customer first in order to get his luck going in the right direction? Very often indeed! This is because many people hope that by ignoring a frustration it will go away.

You can dissolve frustration, but not by delaying it or ignoring it. When we experience all that life has to offer we can become master of all in life.

Good and evil, pleasure and pain, are part of the total picture, the total experience. Total experience is the key to total understanding. You are learning now to include all that happens and then triumph over it by reducing it to its rightful place in the cosmic scheme of things.

When you read a novel, see a film, go to the art museum, or listen to music, you are adding another dimension to your experience. You are not withdrawing, you are *participating* in all that life has to offer. This is exactly what the law of *ideal identity* advocates.

The Law of the Whole and Its Parts

The whole is the sum of its parts and all parts are unified with the whole through spiritual expansion

Once you have alerted yourself to the process of experience, and have started to notice and be in as many different kinds of situations as possible, something will take place within you. By identifying with all, by gathering experience, by feeling along with people, you will expand and grow.

Expansion comes about through identifying with experience. When we identify with experiences we learn to control them, to master them. Identification is the first step. Mastery is next. Expansion and growth is the third step. We expand our total being outward and away from us into all of life, into other experiences, to other places. By expanding yourself mentally, by seeing yourself becoming a larger part of the whole, you gradually become one with the rhythm of the universe. You are one with all things. You are one with other people and with yourself.

How a Stockbroker Used Psychic Expansion for Profit

It was a good day at the brokerage house. The New York Stock Exchange was trading at a fast clip. The Dow-Jones industrial average was up several dollars and trading volume was well ahead of the previous day.

Bill, a customer's man, was studying cosmic attunement with me. He had just put down his telephone after having sold a thousand shares of A.T.& T. He relaxed for a moment, filled his pipe with some tobacco, and looked up at the big board. He looked casually at the numbers changing and thought to himself that he might be able to expand spiritually into that stock exchange board. He did so by feeling as though he *were* the board. He felt the clicking and clacking of the changing prices. He felt the ebb and flow of the business which it represented. Then, without warning, his mind focused on the symbol for a company which wasn't even listed there. Something within him told him to buy.

Bill immediately took out his "over the counter" list of securities. There was the symbol he had just seen! He placed a buy order for 500 shares at $10.00 per share. Before the week was out he sold those same 500 shares for $20.00 per share. Here, through the simple process of spiritual expansion, he had penetrated the workings of the market and purchased a little known security. As a result, he made a 100 percent profit on that purchase. And, he did it within a week.

Psychic expansion gave him the key to the higher power of his own mind.

How to expand psychically

Sit down, relax in a quiet place. Feel your inner self merging with whatever you see around you. Maybe you have a decorative arrangement of flowers, or a book, or a picture. Look at the object, examine it thoughtfully, slowly. Think of its meaning, its texture. Where did it come from? How did it get here? Where will it go when it leaves? Feel yourself *as* that object. Feel yourself as the object before it got to this location. What did it feel then? How will it feel when it leaves?

Next you will be able to merge with the surroundings of the object. You will be able to sense what the nearby objects feel toward the original one. You are expanding through your spiritual faculties. You are merging and becoming one with the things which are external to you. You can also apply this technique in many other ways.

The next time a friend comes to visit, feel yourself slowly becoming that person. Feel that person's emotional state of mind. See his thought patterns develop. Watch his breathing and movements. Picture yourself as that person, yet still be yourself. Observe and participate. Observe yourself and the friend. Participate in the conversation and in the inner thought and feeling of the friend.

You are overcoming the limitations of being only yourself, of seeing life only from your point of view.

You are expanding—and this spiritual expansion will make it possible for you to expand in all areas of your life.

Since cosmic law originates in the cosmos, which is a state of being far removed from the earth, there is a certain amount of dilution of the law as it approaches earth. Mystical manuscripts, down through the ages, have made much of what is called the force of light. Cosmic energy is this force of light, a force that impels life to continue. It is goodness, creativity in action.

How to determine the two forces operating in the universe

There often appear to be two forces at work in the universe, the force of light and life, and the force of darkness, destruction, and death. Actually, these are two aspects of the same force. A diversion of the light force for destructive ends becomes a force for darkness. Sometimes the force of light is used in a destructive way to accomplish good. We destroy disease to create health. We tear down buildings to make way for new housing. We destroy negative thinking in order to have a place for positive thinking. In spite of this, however, mankind has always noticed, and commented on, the apparent force of darkness and evil, the complete malice of some events, situations, and people.

How Martha Handled Harassing Telephone Calls

Martha was receiving harassing telephone calls. Each evening about nine o'clock a call would be placed to her home. When she answered she only heard heavy breathing on the other end of the line. This had gone on for several weeks. She got my name from a friend who had studied cosmic attunement with me. She called and made an appointment. When she arrived she looked tired and completely worn out. Martha nervously twisted her hands and pulled at her dress as though she were picking at lint. She explained what had happened and asked me if I could tell her who was being so malicious

"It isn't necessary to know who is placing the calls," I said.

I explained that she could picture a protective psychic shield around her through which no evil intention could pass, including malicious telephone calling.

That evening at seven o'clock she meditated only with the light of a candle. In her mind's eye she built the protective shield. Then, at eight o'clock she turned on the lights in her apartment and began to watch television as I had directed. She went to bed at eleven and slept soundly for the first time since the harassing calls had begun.

The caller vanished from her life as mysteriously as he had entered. Martha uses this protective meditation exercise once every month and she hasn't had any malicious intention of any kind directed at her since.

The Law of Balance and Equilibrium

The cosmic intent is to bring the force of light and the force of darkness into balance and equilibrium.

The forces of darkness will be canceled out by the forces of light. It is a divine economy that operates at all times to bring good action out of evil, to bring love to bear against hate, and to bring compassion out of sorrow. All balances and all equalizes when the final accounting is made.

When the pendulum swings too far in one direction it then begins to swing in the other direction. The Greeks called this perfect balance, justice. The cosmic law recognizes that *justice is at work all the time*.

The object in cosmic illumination is to bring your entire being into balance with itself. This means mind development, emotional development, physical development, and psychic development.

We all start with the same fixed points, the same cosmic equipment. It is how we build that counts. Harmony can be set in motion in advance of its actualization. It is not determined by outward circumstances, or given to you by chance. You have the power within you to create whatever you desire, need, and want.

How Terry Achieved Safety
in Viet Nam War Duty

Terry at age eighteen was serving in the Marine Corps in Viet Nam. He had studied cosmic law for a short time before enlisting. He was learning to use the psychic mechanisms (or awareness) within his own mind so he could be led into the right circumstances as he faced the unknowns of military life.

What Terry desired, needed, and wanted was personal safety as he was doing his duty. He continued his meditations whenever he could. Each night before he went to sleep he asked the creative power within him to lead him, guide him, and direct him.

The most significant demonstration he had of the law of "balance and equilibrium" was a short dream which directed him to move his location in an open field. "Move, now," he was told simply. He woke up, moved his gear about fifty yards away, and went back to sleep. Minutes later an enemy mortar shell landed exactly where he had been. The forces of light canceled out the forces of darkness and saved this young American.

The Law of Initiation

Any strong feeling, action, or thought, initiates the above-below law into being and it works of its own accord.

Another way of stating this law is:

STRONG FEELINGS *(plus)* A LINK *(directed at)* A TARGET *(equals)* RESULT

When you affirm and direct your emotion toward a target, that which you have affirmed comes into being.

If you think prosperity in terms of your business, prosperity comes into being. If you direct love toward a person, love happens. If you direct hatred toward a thing or person, destruction is the inevitable result. Once you have initiated with all the feeling you can muster, the law of "above and below" is put into operation and the result comes about. This is the principle behind metaphysical healing. The individual is seen as whole and healthy. The direction of this emotion into the cosmos creates the effect of health and wholeness in the person.

THE ESSENTIAL ELEMENT OF EMOTION

Many people are under the impression that "thinking" is enough to activate this law. *"Thinking" alone will not do it.* The thought must be backed by charged feeling, emotion, total commitment of oneself to the objective.

This emotional charge is summoned by two mental abilities. One is the ability to use one's imagination. The other is the ability to concentrate what is imagined at the target in question.

The target can be specific, such as a specific person, situation, or thing. It can be animate or inanimate.

The best results are gained by being nonspecific. For example, if you say to yourself, "I am affirming that this real estate deal go through as planned," you are being quite specific. In fact, this specificity of the target, the real estate deal, prevents the full use of your imagination. What can you imagine? It is all very literally and clearly stated. The deal must go through.

But, if you were to say, "I affirm that success and prosperity will come to me as time progresses," then you've got something you can apply your powers of imagination and concentration to. You can visualize many kinds of success and prosperity, many methods of gaining your ends. By casting through your mind, and using your imagination, you are concentrating the strongest emotional charge at your goal. The cosmos takes up the refrain and brings your desire into being. It may not have been just exactly as you had expected. But, it may come to you in another, better way. By using your imagination and inventiveness, you are permitting the law to operate with the same random, searching quality. The law will hunt, just like a computer, for the right combination of circumstances to bring about your objective. It is inevitable. It is working for you of its own accord. All you do is set it in motion, step back and relax.

How Right Healing Was Secured

"Let my husband be led to the right medical help." With this simple statement began a bizarre recounting of a yearlong search by a woman and her husband for a cure for a rare brain disease.

As she finished I told her that I could not find the right help, nor could she find it by herself but, with the law of "initiation," she could begin the search anew.

She decided to use an item of her husband's clothing as the link. Daily she directed her thought at the link while she suggested that a way be found to a cure. After three weeks her husband was admitted to a well-known clinic where the proper diagnosis was made and treatment started. Six months later he was well. The law of "initiation" had uncovered a new course in the search and one which was absolutely right.

How to direct the entire force of your being for your good

It is advisable to direct your imagination and concentration at a physical link with the target. If you are affirming health for someone, it is a good idea to have an object owned by the person. You can then direct the force of your emotion, thought, and action into the object as though it were the person.

You should be relaxed, ready to proceed without interruption of any kind.

A few moments of deep silence in the presence of the proxy object will get you started. Imagine the health of the person from every standpoint. Direct this health, through high concentration, at the object which is the stand-in for the person. Work yourself to your best possible emotional involvement. Then, release it. Stop and relax. It is done.

The result will depend upon the strength of your feeling and the sensitivity of the target. If the person knows you are going to practice this, and if the person knows the approximate time you are going to do it, he can tune in on the action and gain more benefit from it. He has increased his receptivity to the vibrations which you have set in motion.

If you develop your powers beyond the average level, and it is easy to do so with repetition, the results will be more than you might have expected or intended. That is why it is necessary to be careful not to allow negation or destructive thoughts, or feelings, to enter your practice of this law of initiation. If you were to direct destructive thought or feeling without care, you might injure the person you are trying to help.

It is much better to spend your attention seeing someone healthy, for example, than to spend all of your attention on the destruction of the disease. You might kill the patient along with the disease. You might destroy the favorable conditions you are trying to encourage. Remember that the divine economy is at work balancing things. It is not always necessary to see the total removal of a disturbing element. The object is to create thought which is even more positive than the disturbance.

Protection from unwanted influences

You may encounter someone who is activating this law without care. People sometimes send off negative thoughts without realizing it.

Protection is available for these circumstances. It is possible to gain more and more protection from the sources of light. Along with your development of mystical awareness, you can build a shield against psychic attack.

See yourself bathed in pure white light. See your shield. Watch the impulses and charges of negativity being repelled.

Sometimes people are so anxious to receive impressions that they will accept anything that comes. You can avoid this by affirming to yourself that you will accept only the very highest and best influences, the very finest quality development.

Those who are open to all influences and thoughts can sometimes pick up negation that may have originated somewhere else. They may be the target of someone else's negative impulse.

It isn't unusual for people to complain of symptoms that appear to be like diabolic possession. It is a form of modern-day witchcraft. They have attracted so much negation that they are living with it constantly. Their thoughts, feelings, even their very souls, are not under their own control. They appear to be lost in a fog and moving without a direction. In turn, these people send out further confusion to others who are willing to accept it. Nothing goes right for them. All is in a state of turmoil and upheaval. The mystical student is alert to this and guards himself against unwanted influences by building the shield during meditation.

The Law of Progression and Change

Life's progression is fixed against a background which changes.

The players change but the performance is the same. That is one way of putting it. We change locations, jobs, places to live. But our reactions to things are likely to be static.

True psychic or mystical awareness increases our originality, gives us a variety of ways of reacting and thinking about the experiences we have.

You may have seen a small baby grow and develop through the early stages of life—walking, talking, noticing the world. This progress is fairly fixed, predictable. Most children learn to walk at the same time and most learn to talk in about the same way.

But, there are some things about a child's development which are not entirely predictable. His uniqueness and individuality, his character and personality, are not predictable.

The same holds true for life itself. The beginning point is fixed, birth. The ending point is death. There are a few other fixed points along the way. *The trivial things change. The truths remain the same.*

An Analysis of a Psychic Message

"They are showing me a basket filled with things. It looks like beautiful tropical fruit. Then, someone keeps giving the fruit away to people who are walking by. Each time a fruit is given away, more is added to the basket. There seems to be no end to the abundance," Paul said.

It was one of our weekly group meetings. Paul was being given a message of great insight and meaning. Slowly he began to see what was being told to him. He had much to offer which he should give to others rather than keep for himself. As he was able to give of his abundance, he would receive more abundance. His cup would run over. He had to begin by giving. In giving, he would receive. He had stumbled onto an ancient law of psychic awareness.

The tropical fruit was symbolic of his spiritual selfhood. He had to give inwardly, generously, from his spiritual storehouse of love and affection.

"Now they are showing me the same basket—the same tropical fruits. Exotic and beautiful, pineapple, grapefruit, even some flowers. But the scene is cold. There is snow around me. People are clothed in furs. Yet I am warm and comfortable."

The group puzzled over this additional message. What did it mean?

Then someone recalled that life's progression is fixed against a background which changes. The cosmic law applied. No matter where this man found himself, no matter what the background, he should give of his abundance. It would be returned and the basket refilled even in the coldest situations.

Progression is the accumulated direction of your existence. Background represents the changing events in your life.

You can make an accurate estimate of your life's progression. And, once you have done this, you can build the kind of future results you want and need to be satisfied and happy. Let's see how it works.

How to take your personal inventory

Let's apply this law of progression to see what is fixed for you in life and what is changing. First, ask yourself these two fundamental questions:

PROGRESSION: 1. Looking back over the last ten years of your life, what conditions seem to be always with you?

BACKGROUND: 2. Looking back over the last ten years of your life, what conditions seem to have changed?

Remember to include only permanent states or conditions to answer question *one.* In answering the second question, you will be listing the smaller changes—the people, places, things.

Next, take the list you made in answer to question *two,* and index it this way:

BACKGROUND: • What conditions seem to occur in the fall of the year?
• What conditions seem to occur in the winter?
• What conditions seem to occur in the spring?
• What conditions seem to occur in the summer?

Your life-cycle profile

You have now started to create a *profile* of your life cycle.
You will notice that certain things happen to you over and

over, almost on a predictable basis. When you abstract the *effect* of these accumulated experiences, you will be describing the *conditions* you listed in answer to your progression question number one above.

Now, take the items you listed in question *one*, and ask yourself:

PROGRESSION: • Is this the progress and direction I want my life to take?
              • What aspects of my life would I like to change?
              • What aspects of my life would I like to have remain the same?

With the information supplied to you in answers to these questions you are now ready to apply those cosmic laws which will bring change to you. Having fully understood the principles of the cosmic laws presented up to this point, and by fully comprehending what you are about to learn, you can pave the way for whatever adjustment you choose. By taking this inventory, you know what you need in your life.

Your inner world influences the outer world you experience

You improve your life by conditioning yourself for success. By allowing the positive and creative to take shape within your inner thought pattern, you are attracting a like situation in the outer material world.

First, you condition your inner world, your spiritual self. By setting this inner world into motion, you activate cosmic law. The results of these activated laws are externalized. The right situations and opportunities for happiness, success, and sound living come to you automatically.

Before you proceed, make sure that you understand the laws so far. Go back and ponder them again, if necessary, because you are about to demonstrate a deeper concentration of your mind power, as we are about to present a deeper cosmic teaching.

The Law of Continuation and Conclusion

That which has begun will continue, and must continue, until a result has been manifested.

This law is a statement that what has been set into motion must continue until it has reached its full conclusion. In a sense this law is related to the law of initiation. When a major emotional, mental, or spiritual charge has been unleashed it must reach its intended target. When it reaches its target a new set of circumstances is brought into being. This law can be seen in action in a positive way each day. By picturing in your mind's eye a desire, you set the desire into motion. However, just setting the cosmic forces to work is not enough. They must be kept on target.

How to get psychic activation

Activation is the way you can reinforce that which you have initiated psychically. It is the one certain way to reach the goal or result desired. Once something has been set in motion there are disturbing elements that can misdirect its course. It is like a missile sent into the sky. Data is constantly sent back to the ground guidance system to make corrections to keep the missile on course, so it reaches its target without fail. In physical science this is called a servo-mechanism. It is the correcting device. In spiritual matters the law of activation is the same "self-correcting" principle. It is a mental, spiritual, and psychical energizing of the thought-charge which has been initiated. Activation is done this way:

1. *Repel negation.* All negative thought should be firmly and resolutely sent from your mind, dissolved from your life condition, discharged from your physical and spiritual being.

2. *Dwell on the positive.* Bring positive, affirmative, and loving situations, people, events, and thoughts into mind. Feel them. See them taking shape and multiplying. Refer to the beautiful, the true, and the eternal.

3. *Become neutral.* Let your thought float on the top of the positive vibration that you have set up. Let your divinity grow and develop within you. See the pure white light of protection surround you. See the purple healing ray enfold you. See the penetrating blue light of calmness around you. Now you are ready to activate and direct what you have initiated by the use of your:

A. IMAGINATION
B. CONCENTRATION
   (directed at the link which you have)

The target is bombarded with the force of the mental, spiritual, and psychical power which your emotional energy has been directing and activating.

4. *Set up regular intervals* for work on this particular project.
5. *After each session,* release it; relax, fully; it is done, totally.

The Law of Acceptance and Rejection

That which is accepted mentally, emotionally, and spiritually, gathers itself together with other forces of like character to create in the material life of the individual a complete reflection of that which has been accepted; that which is rejected mentally, emotionally, and spiritually, gathers itself together with other forces of like character to create in the material life of the individual a complete reflection of that which has been rejected.

It is a human tendency to reject much in life, to remove ourselves from it, to avoid the unpleasant. Many people actually feel threatened by anything new or different. Their tolerance for the unknown is low. But, the harmonious person has a high tolerance for the new, different, and the nonspecific. A person who is in tune with the cosmos has a high tolerance for ambiguity, is not threatened by life. This is because the advanced person is strong, firm, solid within himself. Tolerance

for change, for the unexpected, and for the abstract is very
high.

What are the characteristics of the harmonious person? They
are as follows:

1. A sense of the *unity of all things,* ideas, and experiences.
2. An ability to *transcend the material* world and the
physical body.
3. A deeply felt *positive and creative mood* in every
thought and reaction.
4. The realization that *all of life is sacred,* has meaning,
and the opportunity for fulfillment.
5. The eternal sense of the *divinity within* and a high
tolerance for ambiguity.
6. The confidence that *spiritual experiences* are not capable of being described in words, yet they *do exist for
everyone.*
7. Attunement brings a transforming insight and revelation which causes *changes in the outlook, behavior,
and experience pattern.*

*The key to perfect harmony is to be able to accept more in
life than you reject.* Rather than being defensive, waiting for
the worst to happen, you can cheerfully move forward and
upward to a greater understanding of your place in the cosmos.
In this way you will attract all good to you, and you will
harmonize those spiritual forces that are naturally attracted to
your vibration.

Let's see how this works.

Mental acceptance is the reception of an idea, impression,
feeling, thing, or experience. It is also the building on that idea
or experience so that a new creation of that idea or experience
comes into consciousness. In other words, you do not blindly
accept, but accept so that you can create more. Experiences,
ideas, feelings, are the raw material from which your mind and
spirit can extract the best and create something more beautiful,

more unique, more personal than the original idea, experience or feeling. Thus, anything that happens to you or around you can be utilized in your advancement and development. You have made your life a continuous work of art.

The "now moment" of self-realization

Acceptance of all of life's wonderful experience is brought about by inner listening. As we listen we make note of the meaning of the "now moment," the present. We are not encumbered by the shadows of the past, past injuries, losses, or false teachings. We are living from moment to moment as we are guided by what is true now, at this moment in time. We are not frozen, waiting for the fate of the future to bring us something good or bad. We are here, now, loving, experiencing, expressing. Truth is obtained within. It is not measured or evaluated by external circumstances or by a set of standards to live by. It is known by your highest and best self.

When you listen for the inner clues, voices of intuition, revelations of what to do, you are "feeling." When you do this you open your entire being to receptiveness toward all experience, not just the immediate experience in the present. Through the present, or "now" experience you are able to touch all of life since all is unified with the whole. This is the psychic awareness that opens new doors for you.

You can judge each experience individually, within its own framework of meaning. Rigidity of interpretation is no longer a part of your thought pattern. You will become more conscious of the totality of reality as it actually exists rather than viewing it in preconceived categories. This method of accepting and evaluating will actually make you more realistic and successful in dealing with new situations. It enables you to evaluate with greater clarity because you are no longer a victim of past experience or past evaluations. You are able to see the uniqueness of each thing, and, at the same time, you will understand how each thing is part of the totality, the wholeness of life.

Through the methods of weighing and balancing your truest

inner feeling you can reach within yourself, to your divinity, and locate that which is satisfying and meaningful in the "now." This implies choice, freedom, receptiveness, inclusion of stimuli, not rejection of them. Fear of your reactions, your natural reactions, is replaced by a steady confidence in them. You will look less and less to others for evaluation, for the standards to live by. Instead you will find your own forms of expressing life, your greatest creative potential. This is a continuing process, not a final state of happiness or tension reduction. It is not a stagnant insulation from the world. It is involvement in life, moment to moment experience.

By experiencing more than you reject you can gradually know when it is necessary to reject, and you will know how to reject. It is much healthier to begin by accepting, and gradually learn when and how to reject. *The secret of rejection, as you will see in a later chapter, is to reject lightly, and, at the same time, to accept strongly that which you want to come into being.* In this way, you have not energized the thing to be rejected. You have not given a positive impetus to a negation, causing it to double and triple in intensity and frequency. Begin by accepting. Rejection will take care of itself.

The Law of Eternal Life Energy

Eternal life energy is available to all who seek it, and its light sustains life, protects, and guides us through the spirit within.

Eternal Life Energy is the spiritual energy behind all things, in all things, controlling all. It is the fundamental power of the universe. It is the formlessness out of which life itself was created. It is the electromagnetic field which surrounds all objects and people. Faith is the activation of this power, the mobilization of it for our use on the earth plane, as it is on all planes of existence. Through cosmic attunement we are able to be conductors of this power so that it flows through us and remains with us.

This energy is spirit, it is at the very center of your being right now, waiting to be tapped. It is your soul when it becomes released, freed. It is the power behind your Divine Presence when it is operating on a clear channel of understanding and unfoldment.

When you tune in on this pure flowing energy you *do not:*

wish, will, supplicate, coerce, or influence other people hypnotically.

But, *you can fill every cell and fiber of your body* with this renewing, regenerating, health-giving force, if you:

- First, repel erroneous thought patterns, send negation away from you, and *penetrate* and transcend *all subconscious denials.*
- Second, create a positive vibration, by dwelling on the *creative aspects of your inner being.*
- Finally, put your thought and feeling into neutral.

You will feel the energy being released within you, slowly at first, but stronger and stronger as you repeat this simple exercise in quiet meditation each day. Illumination will develop within you, around you, and throughout your life. All who come into contact with you will gradually notice the change, the transformation that this Eternal Life Energy brings. Eternal Life Energy removes the limitation of mortal or physical energy by replacing it with divine energy. Therefore, it frees the spirit of man. Daily meditation of the source of all personal power, the infinite spirit within, which has its existence at the center of our being, ignites the light of Eternal Life Energy.

We can transform thoughts into things. This is the way we create emotionally, mentally, and spiritually. This is the way you can send and direct the Eternal Life Energy. By seeing it in thought, by feeling it in body, and by releasing it in spirit, you resolve it into a *thing* which can be utilized for yourself and others.

Illumination and insight come as this power is utilized and

focused. This causes experiences in the outer world which are directed and dictated by this illumination. These experiences bring the soul into controlling position because it is released to work freely for you. You are guided by your highest selfhood. Transformation takes place and harmony, peace, and true fulfillment work their way into every thought, action, and perception of the world and your wonderful place in it.

Exercise programs to perform

THE LINK, TARGET, AND RESULT

1. Select a friend of yours who needs harmony, healing, or some other beneficial assistance. Talk to this person, explain wnat you are going to do, then ask for an object of personal value that you may keep for a week. Each day at a specific, appointed time, sit in meditation and silence, and then affirm aloud the beneficial assistance for this friend, using the object as a link to the person. Don't communicate with the person until the week is up. Check your results. Continue experimenting with this law, using other target persons, even situations and events involving more than one person.

IDEAL IDENTIFICATION AND MASTERY

2. Choose a day when you have nothing planned to do. Dress in casual clothes and ride public transportation. Just allow yourself to drift, going wherever the conveyance takes you. Imagine you are the people you see. You are the places you see. Identify with all around you. Don't be yourself, be an anonymous person who has blended into the crowd in order to be a part of the whole. Insights will come to you throughout the day. Be sure to go where you have never been, and see people and places you don't usually see. Your mental and spiritual scope and mastery will automatically increase.

PURE BEING

3. Sit in absolute silence and quiet for an hour. Be aware of your breathing, your heart beating, and the blood in your body. Feel the rhythm of your total self, physically. Then picture your oversoul, or higher self, surrounding you, as a soft-glowing light. Just relax and let yourself be totally you. Let Eternal Life Energy surge through you.

Points to remember from this chapter

1. Cosmic law orders the universe and is seen as *result* in life.
2. The system of cosmic law is self-activating since this system has always existed, does exist, and will exist eternally. *Cosmic laws do not depend upon our intellectual acceptance of them in order to operate in our lives.*
3. Knowledge of cosmic law enables the individual to utilize his full spiritual force and ability.
4. Each person passes through distinct phases of spiritual development (psychic awareness) as he moves through the cycles of life.
5. The Eternal Life Energy is a transforming illumination which brings specific evidence of peace, harmony, and attunement with the world, and the individual's place in it.

By now you have begun to see your exciting place in the cosmic universe. *You realize that you are entirely unique.* You know there is destiny at work in your life. There is some-

5

How To Live the Life You Want Through Psychic Illumination

thing that you and only you are destined to do and be. You are using the tools of meditation to bring out your natural power and ability. You are slowly becoming a vital human being with wider scope and deeper appreciation.

You are recognizing the underlying cause and effect of cosmic law. As a result you have experienced clairvoyance, healing, and harmony in your life. You are making use of the natural resource of your own mind. Your extrasensory capacity is growing more and more as you listen to the voice of intuition within. You are being guided and directed in all that you do and say through psychic awareness.

Now you are ready to experience Complete Cosmic or Psychic Illumination.

You are about to transform your life, your circumstance, and your condition. You are about to develop a "way of life" that is tailor-made to your needs, wants, and wishes.

The characteristics of complete cosmic illumination

What are the characteristics of Complete Cosmic Illumination? Here they are—

1. *The Unity of All*—All things are related, all experience, and all objects are interrelated. This is a sense of *your* relationship to *everything* you encounter. It is as if everything that happens to you, every person you meet, and every place you go, is part of a wonderful, infinite plan. The unity of all things is the inner acceptance of the totality of the universe. All is one, you are one, so you are all.

2. *Material Transcendence*—Material aspects of life, objects alone, are not the only goals. The mere accumulation of goods or services does not guarantee success or happiness. The goodness or badness of a situation is determined by the individual in that situation rather than by some external authority or material condition.

3. *A Deep Positive Awareness*—To one who has experienced Cosmic Illumination this is the feeling carried over from the illumination itself. All things seem to be working for the outcome of good. The mood is positive because the results of life are positive, creative, healthy. Everything is seen as working toward a purpose which is fundamentally redemptive. The illuminated person is seldom bored. He is eager to get on with the projects he has in mind and he is able to mobilize and maintain his energy level over long periods of time. His interests are integrated. He refrains from dabbing in numerous areas. He has direction and specific purpose.

4. *The Sacredness of It All*—The illuminated person sees all of life as having a sacred purpose. As a result, the illuminated person does not seek close friendships with a great number of people. Instead he tends to develop close relationships with only a few. But, in these relationships common interests are not necessary. The real basis of the relationship is the communication of deep feeling, or deep spiritual experience, with others who share similar feelings.

5. *Understanding Spiritual Reality*—The illuminated individual sees the world as a place where the spiritual self has validity. This results in an alternation between periods of intense involvement and seclusion. The periods of involvement are used for discovery of new truth. The periods of retreat are used for reflection and renewing of the total self. During seclusion energy is stored up for the involvements to follow.

6. *Truth as an Experience*—Truth is not words or intellectual understanding. Truth is an *experience* in and around those who are illuminated. Intellectual descriptions of the experience attempt to define and explain it. But the experience of Cosmic Illumination is only fully understood by experiencing it. Those who have experienced this illumination do not, cannot, describe it.

7. *A Transformation*—Illumination causes changes in the behavior of the individual. Life takes on new meaning. It is different, alive, and beautiful. The person seems changed because his life's circumstances are changing. It is like falling in love or being awarded a great recognition for a difficult feat. It is marked by enthusiasm, exhilaration, and an excess amount of energy. Complete Cosmic Illumination comes in a series of deeply moving experiences. These experiences are intellectual, emotional, and spiritual all at once. It is these experiences which bring the illumination into being.

The royal road to complete cosmic illumination

There is a royal road to Cosmic Illumination. Many have traveled it before you in many places and in many ages.

It is meditation. *That is, it is a system of meditational exercises designed, specifically, to help you complete at-one-ment.*

Meditation can be used for many purposes. It is the basis for the practice of cosmic attunement of many kinds. However, the deep, *transcending meditation* that brings about union of mind, body, and soul with all of creation requires personal preparation and persistent practice. It is an experience of harmony which takes place *with* you rather than an intellectual understanding or a belief in something. You do not even have to believe in this meditational system to have it work for you.

First, let's see what it has done for others.

A MARITAL INVOLVEMENT SOLVED

Mrs. W. B. came to me with a personal problem which involved not only her husband but her children as well. It was not a new problem to me. But, our solution to it was different. She did not love her husband and she did not love her children. In fact, her interest in them had dwindled to the point where she was carrying on extramarital affairs with several men at the same time. She had a compulsive need to express her dislike for her husband in this way. She was addicted to extramarital affairs and the time had come when not only her husband but also her friends knew what was going on. She needed a way to end the vicious circle of guilt and repressed aggression.

When Mrs. W. B. came to see me she was dressed in attractive attire from a well-known women's shop. She was gracious, charming, and intelligent. Her story was this. She had tried her family doctor who had recommended psychiatric attention. It had not worked after several months of weekly sessions. Mrs. W. B. had gone to her clergyman. He offered to pray and counsel her but to no avail.

Evidently, she was seeing a psychic as a last resort. It was clear that a clairvoyant reading, or a mediumistic sitting, would not have helped do anything but confuse her. Besides, the reading would have unearthed very unattractive things about her thought and emotional patterns. Healing meditation and prayer would help. But, what she really needed was a quick way to come into some understanding of herself. She already knew the consequences that her actions had brought into her life. Through her psychiatric sessions she understood the deep-seated desire she had for her own destruction.

"Are you willing to try anything?" I asked.

"Anything reasonable," she answered.

I began by training her for several sessions in the basic techniques of ordinary meditation, then switched to Cosmic Illumination meditation. Within six months time she was adjusted to herself and her family life.

I did not cure this woman of anything, but simply introduced her to herself so that she became a new person. She transcended her old self and overcame her problem. With new zest and interest in life, she was able to love again. She loved others and, most important, she loved herself.

How a Minister Solved His Psychic Problem

Reverend Bill was a Protestant minister who had just about decided to throw in the towel and give up his ministry.

"Why do you want to do this?" I asked him.

"I'm afraid I don't think there is a God," he answered with a pained expression. The circumstances of his visit were unusual to say the least.

First, he was consulting someone outside his denomination which was in itself a rather sad commentary on his plight. Second, he didn't really know me well and probably had surmised that even though I might be "way out," at least I was friendly and couldn't harm him.

I asked him the usual question. "Are you willing to try anything, to do as I recommend for a period of ninety days at least?" "What does it require?" he countered. "Your time," my standard answer came forth.

We began and ninety days later he was convinced that his people needed him. He continued his Cosmic Illumination meditation and within another ninety days he knew that there was a God. He had experienced God. Ninety days after that he got a call to a bigger, more lucrative church, and today he is a well-known preacher who is gaining national recognition. Psychic awareness developed his constructive approach to his problem.

An Actor's Experience with Cosmic Illumination

Mike was an actor—not a student of acting. He was an actor who made a good living in plays and television shows on the west coast. Occasionally he saw me during his airplane hops to New York. It was after a stint of film making in California that he called me from Los Angeles to say he thought he lacked personal fulfillment. I explained that we all had dry periods and that this was particularly evident in the creative fields. He was an artist in the best sense of the word, and it was understandable that he temporarily reached a dead end. This meant that a new, fuller, more meaningful life was about to present itself to him.

He didn't think that anything was about to present itself to him. He thought maybe he'd take up writing, or painting, or become a bum. He didn't know what to do.

We decided to try meditation for Complete Cosmic Illumination. Mike had a regular regimen for diet and exercise so the idea of adding another discipline was not at all distasteful. In fact he rather relished the idea of doing something for his inner self since so much of his training and time was spent on his exterior self.

Through correspondence we set up his schedule and encouraged him through the various phases of advanced meditation for Complete Cosmic Illumination. Later, we taught him Cosmic Law, ESP, and mediumship.

Mike came through with flying colors. Now he's teaching it to some of his friends in the motion picture business. Meditation of this kind has actually made a better actor of him—and a better person. After years of bachelorhood, he has married and happily so. He seems destined, some day, to be a top star.

How Cosmic Illumination
Helped an Alcoholic

Jack was an alcoholic. He'd been a member of A.A. and was following the program for sober living. He'd been dry for three years and his marriage and job were going well. Like other alcoholics who'd seen me he had a vague, uneasy feeling. He was afraid he'd start to drink again. He came to me and asked what I thought about this fear. It seemed logical to me. After all, what guarantee did he have that he could continue remaining sober? He didn't have a specific reason for drinking again. He only felt that he might. Other alcoholics had described a similar uneasy fear to me. I recommended meditation for Complete Cosmic Illumination.

Jack continued his meditational practice and claims it was the third best thing he ever did. The best was to marry his wife. His second best thing was joining A.A. So, meditation for him is a mainstay in his life. It may even be the cement which is holding him together.

An Unwed Mother's Situation
Resolved for the Better

Rebecca was recommended to me by a physician who had an avid interest in psychic things. She was eighteen years of age, expecting a baby—and unmarried. She had been taken in by a charity and was expecting her child soon. Her parents had not disowned her, though of course they had been upset by what had happened. Rebecca was obviously in need of affection but had tried to obtain it in the wrong way. What she needed was a greater self-confidence; and, in the weeks before the birth, Cosmic Illumination brought it to her. Rebecca reported that new energy and peacefulness had entered her life.

After the baby was born, Rebecca was reconciled with her parents and returned home. She continued her meditations. Rebecca came to see me when her child was six months old and.

again at the end of a year. Both times she was healthy, happy, and filled with real joy. Her family had fully accepted her and the child.

A double miracle had been worked. The child brought love into her life. And, the child brought her a sense of her own value and worth. She was needed. Rebecca gained dignity and poise as she bore her new responsibility. By the time the child was five, she had married and was expecting another baby.

Through her meditation she had uncovered the truth that all things are interrelated and have a purpose just as this child was to serve a purpose in her life. She realized that to judge the pregnancy without considering her circumstances was wrong. Rebecca knew it was not a black or white situation. She was able to realize the sacredness of everything that happened to her, of everything that happens.

FATHER JOHN'S EXPERIENCE
WITH COSMIC ILLUMINATION

Father John decided to visit me because he was being surrounded by psychic events—surrounded because the people who were close to him had been having paranormal experiences. Prophetic dreams, healings, and intuitive flashes of guidance were common. When Father John prayed for people, things began to happen. One woman even reported rappings and knockings in her home.

Father John's healing ability was most sought after.

The "word had gotten out" about him and he was beginning to acquire a reputation as a charismatic man. At first these things didn't bother him. But, as time went on and his fame began to spread he became a little worried. What if he should lose his gift when someone depended upon it? Was it right that he have this gift? Was he really worthy?

Peace of mind was what Father John was seeking and Cosmic Illumination was the technique we taught him.

He not only found a new inner peace but he was able to live

comfortably with the uneasy aspects of being a psychically gifted person. He could discuss his ability without being self-conscious. He could talk with the people who explained their psychic events and remain calm and serene. In short, he had adjusted to his condition of being a working instrument of the higher powers.

How a Suicide Was Averted

Miss F. C. called late one August night. It was hot and I hadn't gone to bed yet. "You don't know me, but I heard your lecture at the Detroit Philosophical Society," she began. "I'd like to see you right away. I'm taking a cab from Grosse Pointe Park and I'll be there within an hour." She hung up.

I waited. I had no choice although she'd arrive after midnight.

When she arrived she sat down on an early American rocking chair in the living room and we had coffee together. "I'm here because I'd like to commit suicide and you are the only one who can talk me out of it," she began coolly.

"Have you thought of an efficient way of doing it?" I asked.

"You mean the suicide?" she asked.

"Yes," I said.

"No, but I'd probably use my sleeping pills," she answered.

"Maybe we'd better start with the reason then," I laughed. She smiled and settled back to tell me of a broken love affair. She was in her early twenties and very much in love with a boy who'd given her up.

They hadn't really had a disagreement. He just decided that he was not in love with her anymore.

"Instead of suicide, why don't you resolve to become a more beautiful person. That would be spite with irony attached to it. You might even win him back."

Miss F. C. began meditation that night and within two weeks was practicing Cosmic Illumination with excellent results. She felt a unity of all things, she was able to set up goals for her life and move toward them, she was positive about her life and realized the sacredness of everything she thought and did. She was beginning to behave differently and her friends and family could see the change in her. Gone was the thought of suicide.

By the end of the second month her biggest reward came. Her former boyfriend paid a visit. They decided to be good friends. Both accepted and enjoyed the relationship on that basis. He complimented her on the change in her attitude and behavior, a change brought about through her meditational practice of Cosmic Illumination.

How to meditate for complete cosmic illumination

During meditation, mental burdens dissolve one by one as wandering thought and the frustrating hesitation of consciousness is relegated to a secondary position. Thought forms from the subconscious, superconscious, and divineconscious take over. First they are abstract and symbolic. Then they are specific. In the meantime, the characteristics of Complete Cosmic Illumination step into your life. You'll be calm and contented, less talkative and worried. Little things won't bother you, and the big things in your life will be adventures. You'll see the oneness of all. You'll experience your true self.

First Week

1. Your meditation room should be clean, quiet, and free from distractions and interruptions.
2. Eat sparingly before meditation, taking care to prepare your food with light seasoning and as close to the natural state as possible for easy digestion. The temperature in the meditation room should be cool but comfortable and well ventilated.
3. Sit upright but relaxed with eyes closed. Watch your breathing to see that it is even. Feet should be flat on the floor and hands together in your lap. Clothing should be loose and shoes removed.

4. If you've practiced regular meditation you need not repel negation or dwell on the positive. Don't think of good or bad, happy or sad. Don't concentrate or work at meditating. Just let your thought "be." Relax. Put your tongue at the roof of your mouth. Close your lips and teeth.

5. Create a pinpoint of light in your mind's eyes about six inches from your forehead. Don't force it. Let it appear, gradually.

6. Let the light gradually grow until it is a sphere which surrounds your entire body. Picture yourself as seated in the middle of the sphere, in suspension, touching neither floor nor ceiling.

7. Feel the power, protection, and energy of the sphere.

8. Feel yourself as the sphere. You are the sphere.

9. Let the sphere, as you, grow until it becomes the world; then the universe. You are the world and the universe.

10. Then, let the sphere reduce in size, gradually, until it is the pinpoint of light. Then let the light dissolve. Relax.

The entire exercise as outlined here should take an hour. It should be performed daily at about the same time for one week.

Second Week

During the second week you can conduct your *breathing meditation.*

Follow steps Nos. 1 through 5 above.

6. Take a deep breath. Hold it for five seconds. Exhale slowly and deeply. Repeat this exercise for the first several minutes of your meditation.

7. During the next twenty minutes examine the pinpoint of light without concentrating on it or forcing your

attention at it. Observe it and its meaning in relation to you.

8. During the final twenty minutes let the pinpoint of light dissolve slowly until it disappears into infinity. Do this slowly.

9. Just before you conclude your meditation let your attention rest on your heartbeat, observe its regularity, be *one* with it.

THIRD WEEK

During the third week you are ready for your *conceptualization exercise.* This is perhaps the most difficult of all. But, it can also be the most interesting.

Follow steps Nos. 1 through 5 above.

6. Observe the meaning of love. Don't think about it or concentrate on it. Observe it. Observe its meaning without thinking of a specific person or thing, or happening, or previous experience. If necessary, think of the distilled meaning of your experience with it. Keep your mind away from the specific. Allow yourself to feel abstractly its full meaning. Try not to think in words or mental pictures. Just relax and let yourself feel the meaning, just pure feeling. Let it grow within.

7. Observe the meaning of Freedom.

8. Observe the meaning of Oneness.

9. Observe the meaning of Light.

This exercise should take about one hour.

You can rotate the three exercises from week to week but it is a good idea to do one exercise for an entire week at a time before using one of the others.

MEDITATIONAL SUGGESTIONS

1. Avoid association with competitive people, criminals, and places which pose physical danger of any kind.

2. Dress comfortably but not elegantly.

3. Regulate your sleep and your rest. Leave time for both. You may read while you rest as long as it is not difficult reading or emotionally charged material. It should not require mental effort.

4. Do not waste your time trying to explain what is happening to you. If you must discuss your experience do so with a fellow student or teacher.

5. Do not meditate when you are nervous or tired.

6. If it helps you to relax, bathe before meditation.

7. Maintain your health and a balanced diet. Drink alcoholic beverages only in moderation.

8. Do not think of good or bad, past or future, positive or negative.

9. Do not expect results immediately or look for telltale signs of progress.

10. If you feel dizzy, stand, move your chair, and change your position in the room.

11. If you feel sick stop for a few minutes.

12. Do not be surprised if you hear sounds or see visions. Simply remain detached and be an observer of the *idea* of meditation. But, you should remain aloof and cool as the experience of meditation is taking place. Enthusiasm is fine outside the meditation room but while you are being mystically recharged your view should be one of acceptance and calm.

13. If you miss a meditation don't try to make the time up. There is no way to speed the process. Just resume where you left off.

The five intellectual realizations in cosmic illumination

After you have practiced meditation for Cosmic Illumination, several realizations will take place in your conscious, reasoning mind. These will take place outside your meditation but will be the result of it. They are related to the characteristics of Complete Cosmic Illumination. The characteristics are functionally true; that is, they are characteristics which are active in your life operating within your personality. But, the intellectual realizations are the verbal descriptions of Cosmic Illumination. You come to accept these as true by your logical consideration of your many experiences.

The five most common realizations are:

1. *Rejection* of the material world as the only basis for reality.
2. *Acceptance* of the spiritual self, or the nonmaterial aspect of yourself.
3. *Realization* that all humanity is part of divinity.
4. *Overcoming* the limitations of the time-space axis, and living outside it.
5. *Expression* of your divineconsciousness as a "feeling for life."

Acceptance, rejection, and realization in cosmic illumination

Cosmic Illumination affects the way you think, the way your thoughts are organized, and the way you accept and reject the things which you experience.

Acceptance is the reception of an idea, impression, or experience. Acceptance is building or creating from the original idea, impression, or experience.

Rejection is the nonreception of an idea, impression, or thing. Rejection is the nonbuilding or noncreating from the original idea, impression or experience.

These two mental actions are polarities; one is positive, the other is negative. Either of these mental actions causes us to categorize since we can put ideas and experience into either one category or the other. Mystical awareness is constantly moving, changing, acting and reacting. It is not a static thing that can be easily categorized or classified in neat packages. But acceptance and rejection can be a help.

Sometimes it is necessary to totally accept or completely reject an idea or experience. But, when we do, we automatically limit our understanding of that idea or experience. When we reject we are actually limiting our own humanity and ability to grow. So, in Complete Cosmic Illumination you will accept more than is rejected. You will also *realize* an idea, impression, or experience.

Realization is the holding away from you of an idea, impression, or experience so that you can later absorb it on its own terms. Realization is the understanding of a thing from its standpoint or within the context of its own unique meaning. This rules out the use of preconceived value systems and structures. It means that each new experience is held in neutral until its individual meaning can be established. We do not say that a thing is good and should be accepted. Nor do we say that a thing is bad and should be rejected. We hold it until it can be perceived within its own framework of goodness or badness.

Realization causes you to be goal oriented rather than situation oriented. You are ruled more by your long-range goals than by the circumstances which occur from moment to moment. Your reactions are regulated by the ultimate rather than the immediate. You are directing energy toward your goals rather than at your frustrations. You initiate action rather than reacting to what others are doing. You are able to adjust your level of aspiration to the realities of success or failure. And, you will choose goals with only moderate risks because you will not be in such a hole that you need a "long shot" to get you out.

SOME PRACTICAL ILLUSTRATIONS

Let's say you get up one morning to go to the office. The first thing that greets you is a cold house. Something is wrong with the thermostat. Then you have trouble getting the car started. You arrive at the office to find a crisis that needs immediate attention. What do you do?

First you *accept* what has actually happened, you accept the experience.

Next you *reject* the idea that these frustrations will ruin the day totally.

You *reject* the idea that the cards are stacked against you. You *reject* the idea that you are inadequate and that your inadequacy has caused the problem.

What do you *realize?* You hold the experience and its associated meanings away from you. Later, you reexamine the experiences and understand them from their own standpoint. You are holding these experiences in neutral until you have a chance to establish individual meanings. For example, later you may find that the house was cold because of a sudden drop in temperature. The thermostat was working. The heating system was just trying to catch up to the change; tomorrow you can set the thermostat for colder weather. The car was slow in getting started because the garage door was open and the cold air came in. The crisis at the office? It was not only solved but turned out to be a blessing in disguise. Your company got a large order from a new customer. You've accepted, rejected, and realized.

Let's look at another experience. You go to the store to buy an extra quart of milk and find the milk has been sold out. You go to another store. The milk is sold out there, too. You go home and drink orange juice instead.

Here is where your goal orientation comes in. Most people would be so angry about not being able to buy milk that they would grumble several times at the store owners, drive recklessly, and be irritable the rest of the day. And, of course, they'd develop a grudge against the orange juice—"a lousy substitute."

PRACTICAL USES OF ACCEPTANCE, REJECTION, AND REALIZATION

How would you use acceptance, rejection, and realization?

First, you *accept* the experience at face value.

Next, you *reject* the tendency to blame anyone for it, including yourself. You stand aloof from the experience—hold it in neutral.

Then you *realize* that the presence or absence of a quart of milk does not really hamper your long-range progress. Your goal is not hampered by the lack of a mere quart of milk. Unless, of course, you allow it to absorb your thought and energy and let yourself waste emotional steam in anger over it. Thus, you are saving your energy for your goals, the things you have planned for later in the day. It is the plans for the day which are related to your goals. The milk is incidental. You initiate the action of substituting orange juice. You have adjusted your level of aspiration to the realities of the situation. There is no milk. So, reality tells you to moderate what you had aspired to. You drink orange juice instead.

The more you meditate the more naturally this orderly process will come to you. You won't stop to think about it. *You'll accept, reject, and realize automatically.* It will be fun because it'll widen your world and make you more flexible in dealing with the unexpected. It is a technique you'll use every day no matter what you are doing or where you are. It is another tool in cosmic attunement that will get you over the rough spots and into really successful living. It will be creative living and worth every minute you invest in the simple meditational methods.

Complete Cosmic Illumination is a state of being in and of the cosmos, the universal, eternal, immortal, absolute. It is a state of highest attunement, harmony, peace, union and oneness.

How to reject the negative

1. Don't reject with such force that the thing you reject comes back to haunt you. Rejection should be easy, almost casual.
2. Generally speaking you should understand the past and then forget it. Do not try to relive it or change it. Leave it alone.
3. Reject disappointment, anger, and frustration.
4. Reject static ideas and conformity.
5. Reject negative statements made by other people.

6. Reject circumstances which speak of evil or wrong-doing.

7. Reject people who speak of negation or frustration or poor motives.

8. Reject failure. Reject suggestions of failure.

9. Reject the "long shots," the risky moves, the big gambles.

10. Reject thinking of the future if it seems difficult or uncertain.

11. Do your rejecting at the moment the idea, impression, or experience takes place.

12. If someone *insists* that you accept a negation say that you do not agree and go on from there. Never allow anyone to foist a negation on you. Return it to the other person if necessary. For example, if someone says to you, "I think that plan would be unwise," counter by saying, "What plan would be wise?" Don't say, "Why is the plan unwise?" because the question implies acceptance of the negation.

13. If you are going to initiate action, rather than reacting to the actions of others, you must see yourself in a position of leadership. Therefore, expect some amount of rejection. You should be accepting more than you reject because you are looking for the inventive and creative ideas, situations, and combinations.

14. When you reject, be sure you know the reason for the rejection.

15. Do not reject yourself, your abilities, or your potential. You have a portion of nondestructible divinity within you which can express itself in your life when you'll let it.

What to accept as positive

1. Remember that since God's creation is fundamentally good nothing can be fundamentally bad.

2. Seek harmonious, beneficial, and positive conditions, people, and places.

3. Accept your own need to have time for retreat, reflection, and quiet.
4. Accept your alertness to your own inner reactions.
5. Accept other people's points of view and seek evaluation of your performance.
6. Accept criticism when it is given sincerely and constructively.
7. Accept ideas which are inventive, original, and fresh.
8. Accept conditions which can be adapted to your goals.
9. Accept responsibility for your own progress.
10. Accept help and love from other people.
11. Accept the unusual at face value.
12. Accept positive recommendations.
13. Accept yourself as part of divinity.
14. Accept things as well as people.
15. Accept thoughts of success, happiness, and fulfillment in your life. Accept the future in terms of success and accept the past as a basis for growth toward your goals in life.

When to realize cosmic illumination

1. The technique of realization should be continuous.
2. A passive state of mind toward an experience is best for realization.
3. Learn to realize each experience individually.
4. Avoid a set of values by which you make judgments.
5. Realize the other person's point of view first.
6. Don't force your interpretation of an idea.
7. Remember you may be wrong.
8. Don't pass judgment until later and try to make it positive.
9. If you are in an emotionally charged situation remain aloof.
10. Avoid personal entanglements.
11. Don't give personal advice to your friends.
12. Time is the best agent for true realization.
13. Meditation is a good time for realization.

14. Be as objective as possible when giving your opinion.
15. Do not express your realization if you are not sure of it.

How to regulate your destiny with complete
cosmic illumination

You are carrying the blueprint of your future in your mind. Whatever is created in consciousness externalizes itself sooner or later in some form. In fact, you can only create in your outer world whatever has been built mentally, emotionally, and spiritually by your inner world. However, you cannot force the externalization or allow yourself to be distraught or nervously excited about it. Some people have actually attracted what they do not want by fear and anxiety about how their externalized wishes and desires will take place. They have attracted further negation, fear, and disillusionment into their lives without realizing why or how they are doing it. Had they been less aggressive and demanding they might instead have been led into new pathways for development and realization. It is difficult, too, if you are under emotional or economic stress, to see objectively the mistakes or imperfections that may be producing the very situations that you'd like to be free of.

Because Cosmic Illumination brings about calmness and serenity it automatically externalizes those stable conditions in your outer world that you need to be effective in your decision making. Actions that are based on Cosmic Illumination stem from the great divinity within and are perfect for every situation.

It is almost impossible to make the wrong move when you are operating as an instrument of Cosmic Illumination. The minute you picture yourself undertaking a new project or effort your mind begins to scan all the people and situations that you need in order to accomplish your appointed task. It may take a little time but sooner or later all the people and opportunities that you need will come to you to insure your success.

By setting the perfect success of the effort in your mind you make it possible for it to be realized in your outer world. By dwelling on the ideal you place into motion an attracting force that cannot be denied.

The Secret of Regulating Your Destiny

The secret to the success of regulating your destiny in this way is to see to it that your mind as manifested through your thought is working smoothly and evenly all the time.

Cosmic Illumination makes it possible for success to be a certainty even though it may appear to be only chance. The object of Complete Cosmic Illumination is the healthy functioning of your total mind power so you are conditioning your mental, emotional, and spiritual instrument. You are keeping it in good working order and in perfect attunement with everything.

A few real-life case histories will illustrate this point.

How Elsie Got the Job She Wanted

Elsie was looking for a job as a medical technician. She had been using Cosmic Illumination meditation for several months as she was finishing her training in medical technology. She didn't want just any job. She was hoping for a job that would be close to her home, no more than a twenty minute ride by bus.

She also wanted a job that allowed her to work afternoons and evenings so she could spend her days with her family. These two goals *were in the back of her mind* during her meditations. The day after she graduated from her training school, Elsie was able to get a job only three blocks from her home and the hours were 3:00 P.M. to 11:00 P.M. She had externalized perfectly what she had been carrying around within her mind.

How a Scholarship Was Secured

Sam was finishing his last year in high school. He was a good basketball player and wanted to go to college but needed extra money to do it. His parents could pay about a fourth of his expenses and he had to earn the balance. Sam was meditating regularly and was confident that he could manage to get a basketball scholarship at a nearby college to pay his way. Although he was a good player he was not outstanding when compared to some of the others who were competing for the few available scholarships at this school. But, when the decision came Sam was included in the scholarship awards. He did well in school and continued receiving financial support as a result of his playing throughout the four years. He also continued his meditations which had proven so helpful before.

How a Home Was Sold to Buy Another

Hazel needed a new house. Or at least she wanted to sell the one she had. She had her mind on a new suburban community. But, her city home was well over forty years old and finding a buyer at the price she could afford was difficult. Throughout the winter she practiced Cosmic Illumination meditation and her house went on the market the following spring. The agent who handled the home was quite frank about its chances for sale—they were slim. But, Hazel was determined to sell it at her price if she could. She was a perfectly tuned instrument, calm and confident. She set the sale in motion in her mind's eye and calmly awaited the right buyer.

The house was on the market for one week. The third person to see it bought it—and at Hazel's price. He was an attorney who had a large collection of antiques and wanted an older home where the furnishings would seem tasteful. Coincidence? Not to Hazel. She knew it would happen that way. Now living in the suburb of her choice, Hazel teaches Cosmic Illumination to a small study group in the Methodist Church there.

What you can further expect from complete cosmic illumination

There are a few by-products of complete Cosmic Illumination. It can help you overcome the time-space axis. And don't be surprised if you get extrasensory impressions. Some people have reported mediumistic contact with discarnate Ascended Master Teachers, highly evolved spiritual beings, on the other side. And some explain that they feel as though they are at the center of the God-Power itself when they are being psychically recharged during meditation or silent periods.

Exercise programs to perform for your cosmic illuminations

EXPRESSING DIVINITY

1. While meditating for conceptualization observe the meaning of divinity. Then observe the meaning of divinity within; then divinity without. Allow your own divinity to express its energy from the center of your body outward, blessing all.

EXPRESSING ACCEPTANCE

2. While meditating, express within your mind the ideas, impressions, feelings, and experiences that you are accepting from the previous day; then the previous week; finally, the previous month and year. Go over each acceptance, recall it to your consciousness and dwell on its significance in terms of the goals of your life. How does each acceptance fit into the total scheme, the total plan for your life?

EXPRESSING REALIZATION

3. While meditating, express within your mind the realizations of the past day, week, month, and year. Dwell on the important ones only. See how they fit into the direction and purpose of your life. See how each realization is part of an infinite progression and plan of destiny for you.

Points to remember from this chapter

1. The conscious, material world is not the only basis for reality.

2. Your higher, spiritual self has validity as an instrument of being in and of the cosmos, the universal, immortal, and absolute.

3. All humanity is part of divinity.

4. The self can be an instrument of divine expression in all that is thought, acted upon and created.

5. Complete Cosmic Illumination is a state of oneness with all. It is the highest attunement, harmony, peace, and union.

6. Acceptance is the reception of an idea, impression, or experience into consciousness.

7. Rejection is the nonreception of an original idea, impression, or experience.

8. Realization is the holding away from you of an idea, impression, or experience so that you can later absorb it with its true meaning in terms of your ultimate goals.

Students of psychology are likely to give Sigmund Freud credit for discovering the significance of dreams. But dream analysis was a tool of guidance utilized frequently in ancient

6

Self-Realization Awareness Through Sleep, Dreams, and Trance

times. The adherents of the Old Religion, witchcraft, speak of it with ease and facility. Sigmund Freud may have developed some new ways of analyzing dreams, but practicing the art has been with us for quite a long time. Joseph's interpretation of the dreams of the Pharaoh is a classic example.

Trance is an old technique, as old as Yoga, Zen Buddhism, the Magi of Chaldea, the Gnostic Brotherhood, the Oracle of Delphi, or even the Kabbala of Judaism.

Today, people are casually asking each other to supply meanings for the symbols of dreams. If nothing else, it is an amusing pastime.

What happens to us in sleep

During wakefulness our body tissues are worn out faster than new cells can replace them. That is why we become tired and fatigued. Sleep allows the body to restore and replenish itself. During sleep our conscious life is at a standstill. The heart beats more slowly, blood pressure is lowered, respiratory movement eases and our muscles relax.

While we sleep our higher levels of awareness are active. Subconscious mind, superconscious mind, and divineconscious mind are free to function without the limitations imposed by conscious thought or the stimulation of the physical senses.

Dreams originate by a process still not entirely understood, somewhere deep within these higher levels of mind. Dreams last less than a few seconds and are visual images unaccompanied by other sensations, except emotion. Often these fleeting pictures carry with them tremendous emotional power. Fear, happiness, anxiety, love, security, the full range of feelings, manifest themselves in dream content. Freud maintained that there were two aspects to every dream; (a) the dream image itself, the sequence of the scenes manifested, and (b) the latent content or the emotional significance and meaning of a dream. He discovered that the language of dreams was symbolic. Dreams disguise their meanings in order to protect the dreamer from recognizing the hidden wishes, thoughts, and impulses which are denied by his conscious life. Carl Jung, a student of Professor Freud, on the other hand, saw dreams as anticipatory thinking, an opportunity for the self to test future actions. Alfred Adler, also an early student of psychoanalysis and psychiatry, offered the explanation that dreams are the compensation for the emotional "hurts" experienced during wakefulness. All can be made beautiful in the phantasy of dreams.

How Lee Interpreted His Dream

Lee R. awoke one night rather suddenly. He'd been observing and studying cosmic law and he had initiated on his own behalf the direction that he be warned of any physical danger that might befall him. Each night, before he retired, he told himself, "If there is any danger coming toward me let me know about it so that I can escape it." He had been feeding this direction to the higher powers of his own mind for about two weeks. He was a construction worker who assembled the superstructures of high buildings. So, the risks of his work were high.

The night that he awoke suddenly he had been restless and unable to go to sleep. But, once he did fall asleep he apparently went into a deep sleep state. He awoke as a result of a particularly vivid dream which he had. He dreamed that he was in Rochester, New York, the site of his next construction assignment. While there, on the ground, he was watching a crane move a large steel beam into place. Suddenly the crane somehow lost control of the beam and it fell toward Lee. He tried to move away from the falling steel beam. He was uncertain about where it was going to land. The more he tried to escape the closer the beam came to him. Finally, with a scream of desperation, he awoke to find himself in his own bedroom.

Lee was so upset by this dream that he could not go back to sleep until he had thought about it. Puzzled by its meaning, he called me about two o'clock in the morning. He explained what had happened, the vividness of the vision, and he explained his own anxiety because he could not escape the falling steel. We decided that it was a warning and took the meaning of the dream at face value.

The next question to be answered was should Lee refuse to go to his Rochester assignment or should he go and be on the alert for such an occurrence? Or, should he actively try to prevent it through the metaphysical use of cosmic law?

We decided to ponder these questions individually for a few days. Since he'd had this warning he might get more on it. I might get something during meditation or in trance. Before we had a chance to discuss it again, Lee received word that he would be assigned to a work location in Virginia instead of New York. In the meantime, others would be sent to Rochester to begin work. Three weeks later I received a long distance call from Lee. He was in Virginia. He had just received a telephone call from one of the men in Rochester. A steel beam had fallen and seriously wounded one of the workers. The wounded man only avoided being killed because he heard a voice, that sounded like Lee's, say to him, "Look out, the beam's falling."

"What do you make of it?" I asked Lee.

"I think that it could have been me instead of him," he said, "and I think it would have put me on the death list for sure. Boy, am I glad I didn't go. I'm going to study my dreams from now on for more advice."

AN UNHAPPY MARRIAGE SAVED
BY DREAM ANALYSIS

Margaret T. had a rocky marriage. She and her husband had been married for about twelve years but it wasn't clicking. They had little in common, little to discuss or do together, and no children. They both worked for a living.

One night Margaret had a dream about an argument that had taken place earlier that evening. It was a little more stormy than usual. She described her dream this way, "We were in the living room apparently arguing with each other. There I was, arms flying, yelling my head off. My husband was arguing back, talking rapidly but without much display of anger. Now here's the funny part. I couldn't hear myself—not a word. I could hear my husband though, everything he said. Now, here is the other funny thing. He was talking about how we met, how we had decided to get married, and how we had enjoyed going to the racetrack during the first years of our marriage. Then the whole thing stopped. I kept seeing fragments of this same dream throughout the night."

Margaret wrote the dream out when she awoke. Later in the day, during meditation, she "programmed" the dream back into her subconscious and superconscious mind. As she did, the meaning gradually became clear to her.

She was being told in her dream (1) that her husband didn't really want to argue with her (he was not talking in an argumentative way), (2) she was talking but it didn't really make any sense (she couldn't hear herself although she was yelling her head off), (3) the key to bringing the marriage back into a happy condition lay in examining the reason they had for being married, (4) in addition, they'd be smart to do some of the things they used to do, to begin sharing experiences together, and trying to create an atmosphere similar to those first years. As a result of this interpretation, which she made on her own without help from anyone else, she minimized her argumentation. She encouraged discussion of topics that led to their going to the racetrack, theater, and other entertainments together. As time progressed, their communication with each other increased. They began *talking* to each other rather than arguing with each other.

After a year of the new approach, suggested by the dream, Margaret reported that their marriage was again intact.

A Simultaneous Dream Analyzed

Ernie and Nancy, both teen-agers, were brought back together because of a dream which they both had simultaneously! They had been dating regularly and quarreled. They both had been studying cosmic attunement in a young people's group so they were aware of the significance of dreams and had been directing themselves to gain personal insight as a result of dream messages.

The evening after their quarrel they both dreamed that they had called each other and made up. They got together the next day over coffee to discuss the dreams. They viewed the prophetic advice as being totally responsible for their making up so soon after they'd quarreled.

Miscellaneous Dream Warnings

A woman kept dreaming of seeing herself in a mirror. This dream led to self-improvement in personal grooming, neatness, and better health habits.

A two-headed goat in a dream gave a businessman the message that his double-dealing might lead to financial ruin. The man was careful in the future not to speak with a forked tongue and returned to honesty in his dealings from then on. He prospered in his honesty.

A dream about a bottomless lake prevented a woman from investing her money in a family business that was failing. Instead she invested her funds in some blue chip stocks. The family business went bankrupt—without her. And, she gained from her stock investment.

How to program your sleep for awareness

The few minutes you have while you are getting ready to sleep are your best program times; that is, you can feed instructions to yourself so that your subconscious, superconscious, and divineconscious minds have material to work on while you sleep. By simply visualizing a thought in your conscious mind with the instruction given to yourself to build on it, you can program the work you'll do as you sleep. Set aside a few extra minutes to do the following exercises as you fall off.

1. First repel the frustrations of the day, the negative thoughts, and fears.

2. Dwell on harmony, peace, and quiet. Direct your body to become relaxed by focusing your attention on each muscle section, one at a time, until you've relaxed every portion of your physical self. Start with your feet and give the following direction:

> *My feet are relaxing. They feel as if they were going to float as I let go of the muscles in my feet. Relaxed and warm, quiet and ready for sleep, my feet are ready to float off to sleep as all tension, worry, and tightness leaves the muscles in my feet. My conscious mind is relaxing its control of my feet. They are relaxing, relaxing, relaxing. They are completely relaxed and ready for sleep—a quiet, restful sleep.*

Give the same direction to the other portions of your body, one portion at a time. For greatest effectiveness divide the body into as many parts as possible. Give the instruction to:

lower legs	wrists
knees	lower arms
upper legs	elbows
hips	upper arms
lower back	abdomen
spine	chest
upper back	neck
shoulders	face
hands	head

3. Now you are ready to start your programming. You should tell yourself that you'll gain guidance through dreams, *or just as you awake,* or even sometime during the next day. This way your higher levels of mind start the process of activating the insight or help that you need. Examples of the kinds of work you can ask yourself to do are (use only one example per night):

Problem Solving—Ask for guidance on a specific problem or ask that you be led into the proper decision. Review the problem along with the alternative solutions that have occurred to you. Ask that you be shown the correct solution.

General Protection—Visualize a protective shield being formed around your body. Direct your higher levels of mind to warn you of any impending danger so that you can avert it. Ask that you be warned of any danger from other people, from your environment and from unseen dangers within, of wrong thoughts, actions, or decisions.

Relations with Others—Direct that you be shown your true relationship to others. Ask that you may say the right things, do the right things, and be the right person full of harmony, constructive thought, and positive loving actions in your dealings with other people. If you have a disharmonious relationship with a person or group of people, ask that it be dissolved and that love and consideration be placed in the relationship.

Self-Understanding—Review your own estimation of yourself. See yourself as a beneficial force in the world. Remind your higher mind powers that you have a unique gift to give to others while you are on the earth plane. Only you have that combination of abilities and talents that are needed to do the thing which you are destined to do. Ask that you be shown the proper way to give this gift, and use the talents and abilities that you have. If there is something about yourself that you do not like, ask that it be removed, or that you be shown the way to overcome the fault or shortcoming, so that it doesn't impede your progress.

Goal Setting—Evaluate briefly your goals for the next day, the following week, and the year. See these goals in terms of your long-range goals. What should you be doing, what do you *want* to do, where do you want to be? Ask that you may revise these goals in a way which will bring the most satisfaction, fulfillment, and happiness to you.

New Opportunities—Ask that you be led to new sources of opportunities. Ask that you be enabled to increase your awareness of these opportunities and ask that your inventiveness be amplified. Ask that the opportunities be fruitful and profitable to you.

Greater Realization—Direct that the workings of your mind be renewed and energized by the Power of the universe. See yourself as a conductor of that creative power, the God-Power, within you. Be a charged battery of the cosmos. Feel yourself as part of the total sweep of events, not submerged by them, not overcome by them, but as a director of events as an instrument of Divine Mind.

What your dream symbols mean

As long as this sleep programming is done simply, without a great deal of heavy conscious effort, you'll enable your mind to dream more often, more regularly, according to the directions which you have given yourself. It is a good idea, as we mentioned in chapter 2, to have a dream tablet beside your bed. Write your dreams down as soon as you awake! Write down any thoughts or feelings you have. These first thoughts are important because, during the day, your window on the actions of higher mental powers is restricted. But, the window is wide open while you are asleep, *and as you awaken, your conscious mind can glimpse the dreams and symbolic ideas which are being born for you on higher mental levels.* It is that half-asleep, half-awake state that gives you the chance to *consciously* know what has been *subconsciously* taking place.

Some dreams are literally true, especially those which are given in response to specific programming and direction. But, other dreams are formulated in response to what you need, your emotional requirements, and what your selfhood and personal identity demand. These dreams are highly symbolic and usually deal with repressed desires and wishes.

There are dream symbols which have universal meaning. They appear among all people of many different racial and ethnic origins. Interpretation of dreams can be easily performed through a process of following the emotional meaning of the dream to its root-source.

Various Dream Root-Sources

A waitress in a local restaurant described the following dream which is a classic, or universal dream. She went into the kitchen. The new cook was there. He asked her something but she could not tell what he said. He became angry with her and picked up a long knife. Finally, he grabbed her and she floated up into the air. This symbolizes her orgasm during the sex act.

What good does it do her to recognize this feeling? As a result of repressing this feeling her reactions to this man were forced and unnatural. She might have even disliked him without knowing why. She could have resented the "power" that he had over her, her attraction to him. When she accepted this interpretation of the dream, she was able to laugh it off, saying, "Now I understand my feelings toward him. It is good to know." The internal pressure which the repressed desire had caused was reduced and she was comfortable. Once a repressed desire is understood, it is possible to deal with it, because you understand what it is, how it works.

Another example of universal dream symbology was told to me by a Marine Corps recruiter. He was married and recently was stationed in a city far away from his home and wife. She was making arrangements to move in order to be with him. In the meantime, he had the following dream.

He was searching for a home. He came to one that was red brick. It had a large center door, Georgian colonial style. There was a large iron fence around the property. There were two small balconies at the second-storey level. He liked the house, but he couldn't get through the locked iron gate. He couldn't get the gate open. The dream symbolized his frustration at not being able to have marital relations with his wife.

The house was symbolic of his wife. A large center door and balconies above represented the female anatomy. The iron fence represented the distance that separated him from his wife.

When this simple explanation was made to the recruiter he agreed immediately. He also wondered why it had not occurred to him since he did miss his wife very much. But, he had not trained himself in dream interpretation. Otherwise, this meaning would have been readily apparent to him.

Sexual desires are commonplace in dreams. So are death wishes. If you dislike someone you may see the person in a death situation. However, your own repressed wish may be disguised. Although the person may die, you will not be the instrument of the death because that would be against your accepted code of conduct. You may watch the death instead, or be present at the funeral.

How to use your dream diary

Let's assume that you have a dream recorded, outlined, on your dream diary. Here is how to interpret it systematically during meditation. First, break the dream down into little sections, its component parts. The smaller the components are the better. For example, you dream you're by a lake; it is blue. You are seated under a shade tree in summer. Your father comes to speak to you. A discussion ensues. The dream ends.

Your component outline might look like this:

1. a blue lake
2. a shade tree
3. you are seated
4. it is summer
5. your father appears
6. a discussion ensues
7. the discussion included _____
   (list the subjects of discussion.)
8. your father leaves
9. the dream ends

Next you take each component and ask yourself—"What do I *feel* about each of these?" What is your *emotional* reaction, not your reasoned answer? What do you feel in response to each part of the dream?

> What do you feel about a blue lake?
> What do you feel about a shade tree?
> What do you feel about being seated under a shade tree?

And so on, regarding dream experiences. Once you've run through the dream in this fashion, put your thoughts of it aside for the time being. Later—the next day, a few days later, or at another time—read your description and component outline again.

When you've read the outline, ask yourself *what you feel about the dream as a whole*. What is your feeling reaction once you've broken it down and then reassembled it, then waited and looked at it after a time interval? It is like fitting the small bits of a jigsaw puzzle together.

A total picture will emerge. The insight and understanding that this total meaning gives you as psychic awareness will add to your own realization of yourself. The meaning of one dream, added to another dream, and another, causes self-realization. You'll be directed by your higher levels of mind because dreams are the doorways to all levels of mind, subconscious, superconscious and divineconscious. Each person has his own set of dream symbols.

By keeping a diary and learning to interpret your set of symbols you'll be able to interpret more accurately and fully. Dreams can be a valuable aid in your everyday living.

WHAT A DREAM
OF A DEAD MOTHER MEANT

Mona dreamed that her mother, who had passed on, came to her and spoke of their family home on the eastern shore of Maryland. Although the house was now sold, it had been the scene of many happy family reunions each summer. Mona broke down the details of the dream and realized that its symbolism meant that she should have more contact with her brothers and sisters. She needed them and they needed her. So, she began to write to them, to call them, and became a more active family member. The family closeness enabled her to express her love. And she gained love in return. The dream led her to this emotional need, this insight about herself. Through it she became a more complete person.

A REAL ESTATE DEAL SALVAGED

Arden was an elderly retiree. After analyzing a dream by the diary method, he interpreted his dream message as one to sell a farm he had *after* he made arrangement for a natural gas company to test for gas. The farm had a rich store of gas and the gas company purchased the rights.

After selling the underground gas rights, Arden sold the farm itself, and this double sale increased his profit by 100 percent. If he had not analyzed his dream, he would have made exactly half as much. The message was obscure and became clear only after he'd broken it down into the component parts and later reconstructed it. But, it was worth it!

Mr. J.G. called, made an appointment and arrived in a very serious mood. He was well dressed, obviously a successful businessman, in his fifties. "My son has been fired from every job he has ever had," he began. His son, in his thirties, had one tragic employment experience after another. Everything that he undertook went sour. He had come from a good family, had a college degree, and the doors of success were open to him. I suggested that Mr. J.G. send his son to me for a consultation.

Three days later Mr. J.G.'s son arrived for his early evening appointment. We got to the heart of the matter right away. He was cheerful, appeared competent, someone you'd readily employ and trust.

"I don't know what is causing this," he said, "but I know enough about psychology to think it is something in my past, possibly several experiences, that are influencing me today." "Why don't we try dream analysis?" I asked. "We have a method that can be combined with meditation to bring the meaning out for you."

After a week's use of the dream diary and analysis system, he returned for a second session. "I've had the same dream with some minor variation over and over for a week," he announced.

"It is about my father. He is in every one of these dreams. A thunderstorm is coming, he goes outside, and tries to saw down a large tree. He wants to get it down before the storm passes by. Otherwise, the tree will fall on the house. It is our house. And we do have a large maple tree in the back yard, the same one that is in the dream. Sometimes he starts to saw only to find that the saw breaks, or the storm comes up anyway and drives him indoors. There is tremendous rain, hail, and lightning."

He felt sure his father represented both himself and his father. He *failed* each time to get the tree down before the storm. This represented the son's *inability* to prevent being fired from each job. In order to react against the possibility of being fired he began to slow down, to avoid responsibility, and to behave in a manner suggesting that he had lost interest in the job and would be fired. He was bringing on the inevitable by thinking of it and reacting to it. But, this did not explain *why* he behaved this way.

"All my life I've compared myself to my father. I've tried to equal his attainment. I always think of myself as second best when compared to him. What I should realize is that I've got abilities of my own that are different from his. I should stop competing with him. He is one person and I'm another. We are not competing with each other. If I try to be like him all the time I fail. I can't be like him. I should be like myself."

This interpretation changed the entire course of this young man's life. Realizing that comparison with his father was pointless, he started to build a life of his own, asserting his individuality and independence.

He started a business of his own. It was a tremendous success right from the start. Today, he is a leader in his community, and respected in his church and civic organizations.

What is self-realization?

Self-realization is the creation in your conscious life of the objective *action* of the *higher levels of mind* which you already possess. It is not adding anything to your personality or character. It is the demonstration of your selfhood.

THREE TOOLS FOR SELF-REALIZATION

Sleep, dreams, and trance are three tools in self-realization. They have one thing in common with each other that the tools of prayer, meditation, and affirmation do not have. *The single factor which all three have is that they operate on higher levels of consciousness. They are single-purpose tools that cannot be diffused or distracted by the activity of the conscious mind!* Since prayer, meditation, and affirmation are activities of *con-*

scious awareness, they can be easily distracted by the demands of our five physical senses. They are the slow-working tools that help condition and adjust our mental faculties for greater awareness. They help us adjust and balance our mystical life. But, sleep and dreams are directly related to higher mind; they are the approach to greater psychic awareness.

How to encourage constructive dreaming

Dreaming can be encouraged when you are emotionally prepared to handle the insight which a dream offers you. If your life is disorganized, disjointed, or filled with fear, guilt, or hatred, you may not be in a position to understand and use what your dreams may be telling you. Dream interpretation works best for people who are ready to accept what they get. This means that people who are in need of help, and realize it, are going to make the most of their dreams. Those who use regular meditation, prayer, affirmation, put themselves into a mental "set" whereby dreams are inevitable.

Dreams reveal the following:

1. *Unresolved Conflicts*—The "sticky" points of our emotions are shown to us.
2. *Repressed Desires*—The things that we'd like to do and be, the things we'd like to change in our conscious life, are presented.
3. *Warnings, Direction, Precognitive Messages*—Our superconscious mind moves backward and forward in time to show us what is taking place, what has taken place, or what will take place. We are given directions based on this reading of past, present, and future.
4. *Mental Rejuvenation*—While your body is busy carrying toxins and rebuilding worn out tissues, your mind is able to clear itself and get ready for the new challenges of the next day. Dreams prepare your thought processes by reorganizing and adjusting your thought and clearing your mind.

5. *Spiritual Understanding*—Dreams are also windows on the totality of the cosmos, our place in it, and the eternal and immortal principles of its functioning and operation.

AN AFFIRMATION FOR CONSTRUCTIVE DREAMS

To encourage dreams, say the following affirmation to yourself during your meditation period (or, just before you go to sleep):

I am going to sleep tonight so that my higher mind powers will open the channels of the subconscious, super-conscious, and divineconscious. Revelation, direction, and insight will be self-realized through dreams. When I awake, I will remember these dreams, in detail, so that I can transcribe them into my dream diary. I am ready to receive dreams about my unresolved conflicts, my repressed desires and warnings. My sleep will be sound, tranquil and undisturbed. My dreams tonight will rejuvenate my mind. My dreams will give me greater mystical understanding of the universe and my place in it. Knowing that infinite protection is always with me, I enter this dream state without fear or worry. I anticipate the wonderful guidance and self-realization which will be mine as I record and interpret the dreams I get tonight.

This affirmation formula will direct your higher mind powers to let you remember your dreams and record them.

Freud theorized that his patients in psychoanalysis had a "censor" mechanism which prevented them from remembering their dreams because their conscious minds were not prepared for the insights concerning their unresolved conflicts, repressed desires, and personal guilts. Freud found that as analysis proceeded his patients could remember their dreams, and he used the material of dreams to hasten their recovery.

As you grow in psychic awareness you will be able to remember your dreams and you'll find them more and more helpful in organizing your life and finding contentment and happiness!

When not to sleep

Sleep is fitful and restless when the body is overly tired. Sleep is beneficial when we are able to prepare for it slowly and carefully. Bathing, a light snack, quiet surroundings, help to still the demands of the day, and prepare the body for sleep.

Take a few minutes to picture a serene setting. Visualizing a high mountain, a wooded, misty valley, a sea shore, or an inland lake will remove the discord of the day. Ocean waves, a moonlit night, or a deep river can trigger thoughts of calmness and harmony. Here are some additional sleep tips: (a) don't expect to sleep right away in a strange place, (b) if you cannot get to sleep, get up and do something until you feel the urge to sleep, (c) if you awaken in the middle of the night, lie quietly, saying your dream affirmation until you fall off again, (d) try to arise slowly in the morning, (e) when you can, take a short afternoon nap—this is important to those of advanced years.

Trance, automatic writing, and astral projection

Trance is a mystery of the mind. We know its marvelous demonstrations but we are at a loss to explain how it works. It is an unconscious, hypnotic condition which can take place without an operator or hypnotist.

A First Trance Experience

Miss L.B. was sitting in a meditation group. She'd been a member for several months. Without any warning, she began to mumble softly. Her eyelids fluttered and her muscles were tense. Her words became clear, "Hello . . . hello . . . Karl is my name and I speak to the subject of the cold in the tank . . . we are following the map . . . and it is cold as we move, thinking of home . . . but, now we refer her to page 500 in the missal book where the message is."

While in trance Miss L.B. had made contact with a former military tank commander who had died in World War II. He had been in love with her. His name was Karl and he was describing the last few hours before his tank was hit by the enemy artillery shell which killed him.

He also had a message for Miss L.B. On page 500 of her missal she found a Psalm which had particular significance to her because it revealed the exact philosophy which he had expressed to her many times when he was alive. *This was an evidential message from a departed loved one.*

A Writing Trance

Mr. R.W. realized that when he meditated at home he had a desire to write. His fingers twitched and he had an intense desire to put something onto paper.

His wife usually sat in meditation with him. So, they sat at the dining room table, in semidarkness. A single candle gave a soft glow to the room. Mr. R.W. put a tablet under his right hand and placed a ball-point pen in his hand. They began their meditation in the usual way with a short prayer and then silence.

Within a few minutes he had slipped into a trance and began writing. He made contact with an Egyptian army officer who prophetically spoke to him of a new military conflict in the Middle East.

Mr. R.W. has continued his automatic writing and has received communications from other discarnates who have accurately predicted world events, given him advice on personal matters, and offered to help him increase his extrasensory perception.

An Astral Projection Experience

Mrs. J.A. awoke one morning to find her husband in the dining room waiting for breakfast. Yet, he was actually over 500 miles away in another state!

She saw him in her mind's eye, not in physical form. But, her mental view of him was real enough that she conversed with him. They discussed a business meeting he was to have later that day with an attorney.

He had visited her, via astral projection, to get her opinion on how he should proceed with his business negotiations. When Mr. J.A. returned, Mrs. J.A. asked him about the strange conversation. He was sleeping at the time and found himself, as though in a dream, talking to his wife in his dining room far away from the city where his physical body was actually lying. Her advice gave him a strategy which made the negotiations exceptionally profitable.

There are many cases on record of the helpful use of this ability to send oneself somewhere else so that those at the second location can see and talk with the etheric counterpart.

The trance theory

The theory behind trance work is one of *misdirected attention*. While conscious attention is directed at one thing, usually an insignificant object or mental activity, the subconscious is induced into the trance condition.

TECHNIQUES FOR INDUCING SELF-TRANCE

1. *Trance Induction for Discarnate Voice Control*—Sit quietly in meditation with a friend. Allow your thought to center on an imaginary point in the sky, such as a distant star. Tell yourself that the more you concentrate on the star the closer you will come to the trance state. Relax. Breathe deeply. Let yourself float to the point as you concentrate on it. Hold your jaw lightly open, tongue out, so that you can comfortably speak when the discarnate control begins to channel through you.

2. *Trance Induction for Automatic Writing*—Sit with a lighted candle, tablet, and pencil or pen. Relax, breathe deeply, concentrate on the candle flame. The more you concentrate on

the candle the closer you will come to the trance state. As the writing begins, continue to stare at the candle. You will emerge from the trance in a normal way, like waking up, when the writing has stopped. Be sure to keep your hand loose and relaxed. Concentrate on the candle flame. Do not allow your attention to be distracted in any way.

3. *Trance Induction for Astral Projection*—Lie down in a relaxed position, breathe deeply. Concentrate your attention on the place you plan to reappear. Focus your eyes on the ceiling, let them close. Hold the destination of your projection firmly in mind—see the location in detail. Feel your astral self being detached from your body and projected to that location. When you have reached the location, slowly feel yourself being reassembled, look around, then slowly move or talk. Make your presence known to those there if you wish to. If not, simply observe.

When you are ready to leave, slowly feel your etheric or astral self being disassembled and return to your reclining position. Give yourself time to adjust to the return before you awake from the trance. The entire technique should be attempted only when you have plenty of time to execute it without rushing or pressure. A minimum of two hours will be needed to do this exercise the first time or two. It may take several attempts before you have fully mastered it. Do not attempt astral projection if you are nervous, anxious, or angry.

How Astral Projection Served One in the Armed Services

Rita and Rodger were a happily married young couple. Rodger was about to be drafted into the armed forces. They had heard about cosmic attunement from a friend of theirs who was a regular at our lectures on mystical awareness. They came to me to get instruction in astral projection since they wanted a rapid way to communicate closely with each other while Rodger was in the service. At first I suggested mental telepathy as an easier way of establishing contact. But, they were willing to undergo several supervised experiments in astral projection. They thought it would be a closer means of contact and a more exact way of overcoming the great distances that might separate their physical bodies.

We started with Rodger. He was able to enter trance but couldn't get his astral body detached in order to travel anywhere. We concluded that he would be a better receptor than sender, so we trained Rita as a sender. She met no obstacles in the procedure, was able to feel herself detaching and reassembling, and returned without any effort whatsoever. She retained an accurate impression of the situation wherever in our trial runs she was asked to visit. They both felt they could proceed. During the several weeks before his departure they practiced. She would lie down in the living room of their two story home. He would relax in the bedroom upstairs. Rita was able to project herself into the bedroom and the two of them would converse with ease. Rita would return and the experiment was over. In all, they accomplished this projection successfully about thirteen times.

Rodger was drafted and went to Europe. They set a contact time each Friday evening. He would rest wherever he was and she would project from the States. Although the astral projections were not as clear as they had been during their practice time, they were confirmed by letter.

Once Rodger felt Rita's presence so strongly that he called her long distance to verify what he felt she was discussing during the astral projection session. They were both amazed and delighted with the evidential confirmation of their "out of body" discussions.

Various Benefits of Trance Demonstrations

Automatic writing gave advice to one study group member who learned about the impending illness and death of a close relative. Plans were made to continue the family business beyond the death of this key member of the family. In another case, automatic writing advised a young lady to break her engagement to a man because he was going to be involved in a fatal automobile accident. She didn't have the opportunity to break the engagement because her groom-to-be was killed at the very time she was getting this message.

Trance work has prompted seeking proper medical attention, led to wise investment decisions, and given advice on personal problems beyond the ordinary.

Trance, automatic writing, and astral projection are little understood but valuable psychic tools. They are not tools for the beginner. But, they are tools which the beginner should be aware of since he sometimes enters them of his own accord.

If you are with a group where trance is taking place for the first time, don't panic, let it run its course. Speak softly to the individual in trance if it seems to help. Don't physically touch the person in trance or demand that he or she wake up. Those in trance wake of their own accord once the material they are to convey is given. Just wait until the manifestation has been completed.

Panic on the part of those observing the trance tends to bring about a possession of the entranced person by discarnate entities that may even intrude upon the waking life of the entranced person. This is a condition that requires firm but experienced casting out, or exorcism, of the possessing discarnates. But for most people who are healthy and who develop their psychic abilities slowly and carefully, trance work can be a rewarding, profitable, and pleasant experience. I have never known of an unpleasant trance experience with level-headed, mature men and women.

When you are ready for trance, it will be an unhurried, easy step in your unfoldment in mystical awareness. You may even find that it is not a startling experience at all. One artist I knew simply went into trance to "take a little rest" and found that he couldn't even remember what took place while he was "away." It was a little like sleeping except he awoke with new ideas and artistic concepts that were pertinent to his work. It was a trance for psychic energizing of his creative senses.

Exercises to perform for psychic communication and awareness

1. *Organizing Your Dream Diary*—Organize your dream diary into categories of dreams. Headings such as these might be included: Problem Solving Advice, Personal Insight, Relationships to Others, Precognitive Impressions, Understanding the Past, Direction, Protection, Suggested Actions, and Greater Self-Understanding.

2. *Astral Projection*—Project to the following places: a friend's house, another city in your state, a location in another state, a relative's home, and another country.

Points to remember from this chapter

1. Dreams are doorways to all levels of mind, subconscious, superconscious, and divineconscious.
2. Each person has his own set of dream symbols. By keeping a diary of dreams it is possible to learn what the symbols mean.
3. By programming yourself before you sleep you get answers to questions and directions from all levels of mind.
4. You can encourage dreams by using a dream affirmation before going to sleep.
5. Self-realization through sleep and dreams is the creation in your consciousness of the active powers of higher mind which you already possess.
6. Trance, automatic writing, and astral projection are important tools for self-realization.

We were seated in my darkened séance room for our regular Wednesday evening meeting.

We had relaxed, repelled negative thought from our

How To Communicate with Those Who Have Passed On

7

minds, increased our awareness of positive thought, and let ourselves become passive and neutral. Incense was burning and we were in a deep meditational mood.

Suddenly a vision came to me —a beach. A man was dying there, people gathered around trying to revive him. Then he seemed to get up and move away, but no one noticed him. They were still trying to revive his body. It was his etheric self that had arisen. And it stood, in the vision, before us. The man began to gesture as though he were saying something. The impression of his words became clear. He was speaking of his daughter. He didn't want her to go . . . go on the trip . . . because it would be best for her to stay and work . . . stay and learn.

It didn't make sense to me. But, in mediumship, one should give the impression one receives, immediately, before the conscious mind has an opportunity to intercede or question. So, as the impressions were relayed to me, I spoke them in a soft voice to the sitters gathered there.

"That's my husband," a woman said. "He died on the beach as you described. He is giving me advice about our seventeen-year-old daughter. She has plans to take a trip but she is still undecided about it. Something has been telling her to stay home—an inner voice. Now, here is her father whom she loved telling her the same thing, to stay at home. It has been confirmed from her father who has been dead for over ten years. It not only proves his existence but it also tells me what to do. I'll advise her to stay."

The beautiful young daughter stayed at home. Some of her friends went on the trip and they were disappointed. They returned ahead of schedule and said that they wished they had *never* gone. She stayed at home and met a new boyfriend whom she married. They now have two lovely children. Her father, interpreting her fate, made the suggestion from the other side, and it resulted in her finding the right mate and starting a happy marriage.

A Profitable Business Suggestion Manifested

"I see a man holding a pocket watch. He has grey hair, a slight mustache, and he wears a dark suit. He is pointing to the watch and repeating the words 'an item' . . . he repeats the words 'an item' over and over. Then he carefully shows that the watch has a latch and it springs open. He presses the latch and opens it . . . several times. Then he repeats the words 'an item' . . . and then 'the item has a latch and springs open.' " It was our regular Wednesday séance. This time Alfred identified the spirit and claimed the message. The father was describing an item that Alfred was trying to market. But, he couldn't interest a manufacturer in it. His father was telling him to include a latch and a spring.

Alfred incorporated this idea in the design of the item and later sold the item to a Detroit automotive manufacturer for $10,000. Here was an idea from a recently departed relative which paid off in dollars and cents. Today, Alfred is developing mediumship in order to get his communications and messages directly. He wants to have regular guidance from the Spirit World and he wants to help others gain the assistance of the spirit entities that they naturally attract.

OTHER BENEFICIAL MESSAGES

"I see a doctor in a white coat who is beckoning." A message to get a medical checkup resulted in the early detection and cure of a serious digestive ailment.

"A woman says that the ring is under, under." A departed wife advises her husband to look "under" for the lost ring. He looked under the living room rug and found a wedding ring worth several thousand dollars.

"Go to the park. Go to the park. Go to the park." A message from an American Indian chief led Marjorie to the park the day after the séance. She met a high level business executive there who offered her a new job as his secretary. She accepted and the new job changed the entire course of her life. Her boss advanced, and she advanced with him. Each time he was promoted she earned more money and finally was able to buy a home of her own.

Psychic mediumship demonstrated in world events

Joan of Arc was guided by mediumistic voices and visions. A poor peasant girl who had never been away from her little town, she was thought by people to be obsessed by evil spirits, until her visions were proven true. She saw herself riding at the head of French armies. The voices told her she would lead France to victory after victory. She convinced the French generals, they put her at the head of the armies, and she did lead them to key victories.

Abraham Lincoln was an active student of psychic matters and held séances regularly at the White House. Mr. J. B. Conklin, an American medium, was reported in the *Spiritual Scientist* as having been a guest in the White House four

Sundays in a row. The result of these special Sunday sittings was President Lincoln's decision to issue the proclamation to free the slaves.

Six weeks before Lincoln was shot by an assassin's bullet at the Ford Theater, he had a dream. It was prophetic of events yet to come and it had a deep effect on him. He told about it over and over to his friends because he couldn't get it out of his system. Each time he told it, he became more visibly moved by it. In his dream he heard people sobbing. He seemed to get up from his bed and go downstairs in the White House. He searched from room to room for the invisible mourners. He finally entered the East Room. There was a catafalque, and a corpse in full funeral attire. Soldiers were stationed as guards.

A group of mourners stood weeping. Mr. Lincoln asked, "Who is dead in the White House?"

"The President," was the reply. "He was killed by an assassin."

The President looked at the man in the coffin whose face was covered as if to hide a wound.

Was Abraham Lincoln a spiritualist?

In 1891, Nettie Colburn published a book about her sittings for Abraham Lincoln. A medium herself, Nettie entitled her book Was Abraham Lincoln a Spiritualist? Spiritualism was a popular means of gaining guidance and direction during Lincoln's time. And, no doubt the President had psychic ability and encouraged sittings in order to better know the truth. But, he never formally identified himself with the movement, and it would be wrong therefore to call him a Spiritualist. Nevertheless his interest in Spirit and in Spirit teachings cannot be seriously doubted.

Mediumship beginnings

How did communication with those who've passed on come into being? The Bible speaks of it. The American Indians practiced it. It is a popular religious activity in many parts of the world. Modern Spiritualism began on Friday, March 31, 1848. In Hydesville, Wayne County, New York, two sisters, Margaret Fox, fifteen years of age, and Kate, twelve, heard strange rappings at night. The sisters found that these rappings would respond to their request. "Count one, two, three, four," they asked. The entity behind the rappings did so immediately. A code evolved for "yes" and "no." They asked if the rapping was produced by a spirit. The answer was two raps, the code for "yes." They developed a method of spelling out the letters of the alphabet. It turned out that the spirit was a man who had been murdered in the house. Later, his body was unearthed in the basement exactly where he had said it was buried. Public reaction was spontaneous and loud. The Fox family was deluged by requests to see the girls and hear the rappings. They were subject to both ridicule and reverence. Their neighbors spoke in favor and against. Visitors never really could agree. It must be a trick. It can't be a trick. It is legitimate. It is not legitimate. And so the controversy intensified.

By 1852, only four years later, the movement known as Spiritualism had its first nationwide convention in Cleveland, Ohio. Some commentators called it a social and religious revolution. It "caught on" to say the least. Mediums were being discovered everywhere. Frauds were common. Genuine ghosts were talking to thousands in parlors all over America. There was no end to the quest to understand, to know for sure, and to duplicate the results of others.

What is a true medium?

A medium is an instrument through which discarnate souls express themselves. But, a medium is much more. A medium is able to sense and direct spiritual forces and energies. That is why some mediums demonstrate an entire range of extrasensory ability. Almost everyone has some mediumistic ability though it may be latent. For some, it is not strictly a matter of communicating with the other side. It may be a greater awareness, an ability to cast forward in time as well as backward. It may be the capacity to "see" an event before it has taken place because events cast their shadows in the present. Or, to put it another way, the present is the parent of the future. So, by reading the present, we see the future.

Mediums often look for the meaning underneath the surface of things. They are critical to the extent that they do not accept the superficial, the obvious, the mundane. They understand the deeper meanings as a result of knowing the deeper teachings which are given to them by the Spirit World.

Predictions of future events

The death of Cardinal Spellman was forecast ahead of time in a psychometry demonstration at a regular Sunday Service. A woman that I know named Cecelia, a devout Roman Catholic, placed an envelope in the tray. It turned out to be an object from the famous Italian priest-stigmatist, Father Pio. I clutched the envelope and began to see the funeral of a high ranking prince of the Roman Catholic Church. It was a Requiem Mass. I described the movements and the setting. Finally, I could distinguish St. Patrick's Cathedral in New York City. "It must be Saint Patrick's," I said. "And, the man is Cardinal Spellman."

How to develop mediumship

Developing mediumship is not necessarily a slow process. It does require effort and an investment in your time, especially in your quiet time. Mediumship, like other psychic abilities, is an experience rather than a belief. Mediumship proves itself to you. It is a discovery in the laboratory of your own life. It comes to you as you seek it out. There are certain intellectual insights which usually accompany mediumship. These are realizations, the rationale, behind the phenomenon which enters your life as you are ready for it. For beginning mediums, it helps to understand this rationale at the outset. This basic understanding will help you explain the fascinating and wonderful experiences that you will have as you progress in mediumship. Here are the Nine Fundamentals of Spirit Understanding. These fundamentals underlie most mediumistic experience. And as we explain the techniques of how to develop your mediumship you'll see how this fundamental explanation will guide you. These Nine Fundamentals will come to your mind again and again as you encounter more intricate messages from the Spirit World.

Nine fundamentals of spirit communication

1. God exists. God is Divine Mind or Infinite Intelligence or the God-Power of the Universe.
2. God-Power demonstrates itself in our lives continually.
3. The God demonstration is through the Spirit, or Soul, within us. God's Presence of Light, Life, and Love, is the Healing, Redemptive Force which was in Christ, and in all great spiritual leaders.
4. The Spirit, or Soul, within us grows and develops as we become aware of its existence and how it responds according to natural laws of its own.
5. We can encourage the development of our spiritual selfhood by putting ourselves in touch with other Spirit Beings who are interested in us and in our progression and development.
6. When we are in communication with highly evolved Spirit Beings we become channels, or instruments, through which the God-Power can operate in our lives.
7. Our first contact with the Spirit World is the most important. The first entity, or Guide, is able to bring in others who are on his level of development or who are in a similar state of awareness.
8. It is necessary to prepare our minds, bodies, and souls for the reception of guidance, direction, and assistance from these highly evolved Spirit Beings so that their vibrations can reach us in pure form.
9. When we are prepared through prayer, meditation, and study we make it possible for the Spirit World to inter-

sect our world and help transfer Harmony, Peace and Fulfillment into this life, at this time, for all sincere seekers of Truth. Thus, we are instruments of the God-Power, and all who come in contact with us are touched by this God-Power and its Harmony, Peace, and Fulfillment.

First steps in psychic sensitivity

The first step in mediumship is to establish regular, reliable contact with the Spirit World. This can be done through another medium who tutors the student. It helps to go to meetings where spirit contact is discussed and demonstrated and it is a good idea to visit with psychic people of all kinds since there seems to be a relationship between all of the psychic gifts.

If you meditate on a planned basis you can establish contact by visualizing a person in the Spirit World. You set up a "call" for this person and you can attract him to you. Once you have the contact you mentally ask questions: Are you willing to help me? Can you direct me? Are there others whom I should contact? What should I do next in my development? Can you bring others to me as evidence of survival?

Encourage a conversation with this person. After more effort, you may find, as Arthur Ford, famous American medium found, that someone you don't know will come through and become a permanent guide or link with those on the other side. You may have started with someone you know well, a friend or relative, and you gradually build the vibration, the spiritual strength, to make contact with your permanent guide or channel.

Your Inner Band and your Outer Band for psychic communication

As you increase your communication with discarnates you will find that you attract certain ones with regularity.

The Inner Band is small in number, maybe five, or seven, occasionally nine. This group is usually led by one very strong person who acts as the guide to bring in the others. This group usually consists of friends, relatives, and those who have a particular interest in the individual or through a love tie or a mutual interest are "naturals." Usually the guide is highly evolved, may lead several lives, and is a strong power force for the others rather than being an "information" channel on his own. Frequently the actual identity of this personality may not be known for a long time. For the beginning student it may appear that the messages are coming directly from the other members of the Inner Band when actually they are being translated through this guide. This accounts for the preponderance of American Indians in this role—and other "silent" people.

The Outer Band is a more highly specialized and Ascended Group. Here the range of possibilities becomes very great, and the work these people do is basically spiritual in nature. The number in your Outer Band is usually larger than in the Inner Band. They tend to be more exotic and unique as far as their interests go, but often their identity as individuals is more difficult to ascertain and their personalities tend to merge.

You may start out with one set of outer guides, and find, as you become more spiritualized, that you come in contact with higher and higher forces. One entity seems to lead to another in a very abstract and yet still specific way.

Occasionally a member of your Outer Band seems to work so closely with you that he or she becomes a permanent part of your development and becomes for all intents and purposes part of your Inner Band. Then the identity and personality of the discarnate becomes more obvious and strong evidential detail is forthcoming. Most students who are well developed find that their Inner Band is almost totally taken up with these "strangers who are specialized" and help not only with individual progression but with the details of living.

As you progress and learn the meaning of symbology, you will find that you will get impressions from both of these groups. The evidential messages come usually from your own loved ones who have passed on and "reside" in the Inner Band. This proves to you that they are there waiting for you to welcome them further into your life and action. At the same time you will get Outer Band messages which are more abstract, more spiritual, and in many cases, are intended for others whom you know.

How Messages Are Communicated

Messages don't come in one, two, three order. They are mixed—some here, others there. They might be:

    a. messages identifying the person who is speaking
    b. messages about your own spiritual development
    c. messages warning you or suggesting a course of action to take
    d. power, protection, and guidance messages to help sustain you through your life

It takes, sometimes, several sittings to get the full meaning of a message. And, often, it is a cross-correspondence message. That is, part of it comes from one person, part from another, at different times or places.

You will find that communication with those who have passed before you is a natural expression of love. They are interested in your growth and development. And, you are interested in their progression. You will find that as Spirit Beings pass through their own stages of evolvement they become more and more different from the way we remember them. They grow and develop on the other side much as we do here. They may be less interested in our affairs and more interested in our refinement as spiritual instruments as time passes.

What happens to spirit beings?

A question you'll want to answer for yourself is: What finally happens to spirit beings as they develop on the other side?

They seem to progress through levels of awareness or planes of existence until they return to Divine Mind or God. They return to their point of origin. They merge into the God-Power and work less as individuals and more as a group of Ascended Master Teachers. In the meantime, they are able to act clairvoyantly, transmitting the light of healing and the energy of strength and love to those of us still here on the earth plane.

Finding a development group

Probably the most exciting method of developing mediumship is with other like-minded people. There are so many such small groups in the United States today that it almost seems that a spiritual underground is operating to bring about a renewal of spiritual gifts of all kinds. Even the staid Protestant denominations are holding "sittings" to learn how to pray, how to meditate, how to heal, and how to develop extrasensory perception and mediumship. Spiritual Frontiers Fellowship is an interdenominational Protestant group which sponsors such group study. Finding just the right group may be a little tricky. Many groups start with assumptions that are hardly universal or open minded. There is often one bias or another. But, if you locate a group of loving people who are inquiring rather than trying to gain converts, you've had good fortune. You may initially stumble upon such a group in your random search. If you don't find such a group, you may want to form one with friends who have expressed an interest in psychic matters. If you do this, be sure to meet regularly, preferably once a week for about two hours. You'll want to choose a quiet location free from interruptions or noise. Here is a method of receiving spirit that has worked excellently in our groups. This is a genuine "how-to" method that invariably gets results. It can work for your group, too.

How to receive in a development group

1. Have a formal but sincere prayer and a Bible reading at the beginning of each meeting.

2. Meditate silently for a reasonably long period of time in the dark.

3. Finally, go around the circle, each member giving a full description of his impressions, and his interpretation, if any.

   The other members of the group re-create in their minds the impressions being described and then give, as they are led, their own interpretations, embellishments, and additional impressions which they've built from the original description.

4. Continue around the room and recite the original impressions. However, speak at random as the spirit moves you in your interpretations of these original impressions.

5. The idea is to operate in a nonstructured, spontaneous way, without a sense of step-by-step formality. Free-flowing is the best description of this part of the procedure. Assume that each member is just as capable of being a spiritual instrument as the next member. Allow the full flowering of each individual's ability without imposing restrictions or arbitrary rules. In other words, say what you feel, tell what you get, give what you see, no matter how insignificant or unimportant it seems. The unimportant turns out many times to be the *most* important in the long run.

Verifying messages

Accurate extrasensory forecasts are referred to as "evidential impressions." Mediumistic messages are also called evidential when the person doing the communicating from the other side can be identified by the message. In order to be truly evidential the content of the message must be such that no member of the group could have known of it ahead of time, except, of course, the person who can verify it. In other words, the medium conveying the message should have no empirical method of gaining the message except through a discarnate entity. All other means of knowing the message must first be ruled out so that only the intervention of a discarnate remains as the explanation.

Interpretation

Once impressions begin to flow freely, accurate group interpretation becomes the focal point for further development.

Once an impression is described, *first* reactions should be given, no matter how fleeting or even silly they may seem. The reason is that there is no single interpretation. There is no good interpretation or bad interpretation. All impressions are, until a group interpretation is arrived at, *equal in value*. Everyone has just as valid an interpretation as the next person.

You may *only feel* a certain way about the described impression. You may get *more detail* on it. Or, you may get a *fresh impression*. Whatever you get, *share it*.

It may help to offer your interpretation of someone else's impression along with a question or two for clarification. For example:

> *"I don't believe that impression is for me, but I think there is something significant in the last portion, would you mind repeating it."* (retelling)
>
> *"Did you have any feelings about this impression when you got it?"* (emotional content)
>
> *"Do you think this might be a symbol of identification from someone in your band, or is it for someone else who is here?"* (identification)
>
> *"Does this impression relate to something you are doing now?"* (current action)
>
> *"Does this impression relate to another impression you've had recently?"* (previous impression)
>
> *"Does this impression suggest a course of action to you, something you should or should not do?"* (course of action)
>
> *"Are you sure about the color, shape, place, person?"* (verification)
>
> *"Does this impression relate to another one that someone else has given today?"* (group verification)

> *"Can you tell who this impression might be coming from?*
> (identification)
>
> *"I think that impression is related to me somehow, but I
> don't know for sure, would you say that the* _____?"
> (individual verification)

Building the vibration

You'll notice that people who are psychic talk of the "vibration." We speak of the vibration, the wave length, on which a friend, relative, or guide from the other side comes through. Building the vibration means creating those conditions which make reception good and clear. Some methods of preparing and building the vibration for clear reception of messages from the Spirit World are:

1. *Music.* Singing or playing an instrument always brings a good vibration. Soft, recorded music helps, and so does a round or two of "oahms" or humming by members of the group.

2. *Fresh Flowers.* Flowers seem to encourage Spirit Beings. Some people have developed the art of psychometry with flowers. It is possible to use a fresh flower as a contact point or method of receiving a message from the Spirit World. By contact with a flower while the mind is in a passive, neutral, receptive state, the impression comes through on the blank motion picture screen of the inner mind.

3. *Incense.* A rare blend of incense, burning during a meditation or while a group is seeking, is an excellent way to clear the channels to the Spirit World and build a positive vibration.

4. *Humor.* All mediums are not serious people all of the time, and a light touch with psychic development can help in a positive way that no amount of long-faced prayerizing can equal. After all, those on the other side still have their sense of humor too. There is no need to approach a sitting as though the world were about to end. It may be just beginning.

5. *Rest*. The best, most evidential messages, seem to come through those people who are well rested, harmonious, and quiet. The poorest reception is usually associated with a fragmented, tired, cranky medium. So, if it is good mediumship that you want, get your rest, your sleep, and your meditation, without fail.

6. *Recreation*. Our best development groups spend leisure time together. They go to the movies, to concerts, to lectures, and to parties with each other. They invite each other to dinner and encourage discussion and intellectual stimulation of all kinds. They go to sporting events together and they play tennis, golf, and pool together. In other words, they increase contact with each other in a helpful, moving, sharing way, in addition to their mediumship. Mediumship is part of life but not the total of it or even the largest part. It is a natural thing which can be blended with business, recreation, and other intellectual and cultural activities.

7. *New Sitters*. Nothing revitalizes a group as much as an occasional guest participant or observer or even a new member for the group. New people bring new contact with the other side. They add to the dimension and increase the positive vibrations of the group. No group should be exclusive or it will die. Including new people is an excellent way to keep the interest of the sitters and the communicators at a high level. The evidence increases and the benefits of the message work become more and more obvious as new sitters are gradually included.

How to question the guides

"How can you be sure that that came from my mother?" a man asked me after a private sitting one Saturday morning. He had asked her about his impending move to Florida. He was about to retire and wanted her advice on where to settle.

"Are you sure she is the one to consult about this move?" I had asked. He replied that she was the only one he knew in the

Spirit World whom he felt confident about. And, he had had several previous contacts with her, principally through his own dreams. We decided to try contacting her. He brought an object sealed in an envelope which had belonged to her and had great significance to her. We learned later that it was her wedding ring that he'd inserted in the envelope.

I felt contact with her. I described a woman that I saw and then got a phrase, "In love with fidelity." Charming, I thought, but not too meaningful. But, as I mentioned this phrase, the sitter opposite me changed his position in his chair quite noticeably. "Is there something wrong?" I asked.

"No," he replied. "Except, the inscription on my mother's tombstone is, 'In love with Infinity.'" I felt we had made some definite contact with her.

"She advises central Florida, central in terms of east and west, and central in terms of north and south," I concluded.

She seemed to vanish from my view. It was then that the man posed the question of the true identity of the communicator. We made three suggestions on how to question this communication.

First, we suggested that he submit the question to his mother just before he went to sleep. Apparently he could contact her in this way because he had done so before.

Second, we suggested seeking another medium for verification. If his mother had issued this communication through me she surely would do so through another.

Third, we suggested he submit the question in a sealed envelope to his development group. The objective here was to see if another member of the group could get the same message, possibly in slightly altered form.

The sitter used all three of these methods of questioning and received positive verification each time. He submitted the question before retiring one night and saw a map of Florida with the city of Orlando clearly marked. Another medium saw his mother, described her in detail, and told him he should go to a "place with a middle." In his group he received descriptions of semitropical vegetation and references to the "center" of "activities." He concluded that these additional communications verified his original sitting with me. He settled in central Florida and is very happy.

When not to communicate

Don't try to make contact when you are tired or irritable, when you are ill, or when you are under stress from other people. Mediumship, like other forms of extrasensory perception, works best when it is not pressed into service under adverse conditions. It is an art of indirect attention and cannot be forced or coerced to your will or anyone else's. In other words, don't push yourself beyond your limits. There will be times when you cannot establish evidential contact. When this happens, simply stop for the time being. There will be times when you feel crowded. Stop. Rest. Relax. And wait until conditions improve.

Exercises to perform

BUILDING YOUR BAND OF GUIDES

1. Once you've established spirit contact send out the thought that you'd like additional entities to show themselves to you and help in the development of your mediumship.
2. As you go to sleep, pray that your guides may be made known to you in ever increasing numbers and that they may make an instrument of your life and work.
3. Be on the lookout for signs and signals that the Spirit World is trying to reach you during your waking hours in ways that you may not have thought of before. Many times *they* may be trying to reach *you* and you are not receptive. So be prepared to welcome these visitors when you least expect them, particularly when you are alone.

SUBMITTING QUESTIONS TO SPIRIT

Submit questions to Spirit by simply asking yourself the question. For example, say to yourself, "I wonder if I should go to _____? I wonder if this is the right investment? Should I sell this property? Should I date this girl? Should I go to school here? Should I do this or that?"

By consciously submitting these mental questions to Spirit you will be led to make the right choice and move in the right direction.

RECEIVING HEALING AND ENERGY

While you are sitting alone in meditation allow the Spirit World to gather round. See them. Sense their presence. Then ask for healing, protection, and harmony. Feel every fiber of your body and mind being energized and renewed, recharged, by the spiritual energy which is flowing into you. Repeat this exercise each day for an entire week. Then notice the extra lift and fresh approach it gives your thought and action. Notice how this energy comes to you when you need a second wind or added boost. Each decision you make will be given further power by the spiritual energy which has been flowing through you. Notice the tension and worry dissolve. See and feel the lightness and ease with which you move through each day. Call on the Spirit World when you have a difficult task to perform or an important decision to make.

Points to remember from this chapter

1. Communication with those who have passed on is a natural expression of love. They are interested in us just as we are still interested in their further progression.

2. As Spirit Beings pass through stages of development they become somewhat different from the way we knew them and they begin to merge and work with other more Ascended Master Teachers.

3. Spirit Beings return to Divine Mind from whence they came. Until they become part of the God-Power again they are able to act clairvoyantly and can transmit the light of spiritual energy and insight to those of us still here on the earth plane.

Negative thought forms can be just as effective as positive thinking. When it comes to mind over matter, destruction or working of malice is possible!

How To Protect Yourself from Psychic Attack

Modern medical science is beginning to notice the tremendous influence of thought on health. Psychosomatic medicine is devoted to the relationship between our thought and our physical health.

The impact of thought forms upon you

It is easy to see how our *own* thought can influence our bodily functions. What appears even more astounding, at first, is that we can also be influenced by the thoughts of *other* people, wittingly or unwittingly! But, each day of our lives, we are bombarded by the thoughts, communications, feelings, and desires of other people. Some people know exactly what they are doing. The advertising industry has studied ways to influence our decisions and even our hidden desires. It can manipulate the sales of large quantities of goods and services by appealing to our innate needs. There are many people who are unaware of the effect they have on other people. They send out thoughts of a destructive character. These mysteriously negative thought patterns join with other malicious thoughts to create a negative cause and effect chain reaction with enormous energy behind it. Whole communities and societies can be the victims of escalating mistrust and "bad luck" brought on by suspicion and hatred which have been generated by its leadership.

Three classic cases of malicious psychic attack

Miss R.B. called me to report that a purposeful, planned psychic attack was being waged against her by several persons. She had become the target of a malevolent pattern of thought by three women who were jealous of her. They not only aggressively spoke ill of Miss R.B. but also assaulted her character with unsigned notes sent to her personally. They even went so far in intruding on her privacy that they wrote vicious letters to her employer and to the landlord of her small rented home.

At my suggestion Miss R.B. visited me and unraveled the story a little more. She was a small woman in her early thirties. She had never been married but was attractive and had several regular gentlemen friends. It was her free and easy manner, friendly smile, and single status which had aroused the three ladies to such a fever pitch of vicious intrusion.

Miss R.B. worked as a stenographer in an office attached to a steel mill. As might be expected, the jealous women were wives of three men whom she had met at work. She was as friendly to them as she was to everyone she met. She was not overly friendly, however, and certainly had not dated any of these married men. But, somehow, the rumors had started and as they ground on, Miss R.B. was swept into the role of a "flirting woman" who endangered marriages. The situation had reached a crescendo of charge and countercharge with the three wives teaming up against her.

At first she did not mind the rumors. A certain amount of that was par for the course in her little company. But the turn of events was preventing her from sleeping regularly. She was tense and overly nervous most of the time. She felt guilty even though she had nothing to feel guilty about. It was causing her to make errors. Her thinking wasn't as clear as it had been. Her perception of herself was becoming cloudy. She found decisions difficult to make and she often changed her mind about something in midstream.

Her case was classic. It bore the earmarks of malicious psychic attack. There was nothing accidental about it. The individuals in question felt that Miss R.B. was a threat and they wished, willed, her destruction by any means possible. Miss R.B. was getting headaches that were blurring her vision.

Let's take a look at two other classic cases.

How Sydney Was Worked Upon

The case of Sydney G. also shows all the earmarks of malicious psychic attack. Sydney was a successful businessman. His astuteness and quick response to emerging deals which he could "buy into" made him nearly a millionaire. He dealt in used equipment for the construction industry. He readily admitted that his success had made some enemies, several of whom tried to best him just for the sake of proving that they could beat him at his own game. He explained to me that at least two of these disgruntled competitors would work together to undercut his bid on the equipment that he attempted to sell. He had reason to think that they were working together to put him out of business and they frequently would sustain small losses just to hasten his downfall.

Sydney G. certainly was not a weak man. He was the type to welcome competition. But this concerted effort to do him in was beginning to disturb him. He was slowly beginning to lose confidence in his own ability. What was bothering him more than anything else was the fact that some dealers with whom he had frequently done business were giving him a cold shoulder. In some cases others did business with him reluctantly. Some refused to do business at all. His credit rating was being questioned. His ability to deliver what he promised was under scrutiny. It seemed as though some omen of impending doom or failure was preceding him wherever he went. He found that he was making poor judgments, obligating himself to risks that were too high. He was out on a financial limb more times than he cared to admit. Things could not go on much longer in this way.

How Sophia Was Psychically Disturbed

Sophia was our third case that fitted the classic mold. She was a widow in her late fifties. Her husband had passed on about ten years prior to her having been admitted to one of our study groups. She had the feeling that discarnate entities were tugging and pulling at her. They woke her up at night, gave her pain in her back and made it difficult for her to walk. Her doctor could not find the physical cause of the back pains. She hesitated to tell him she felt that it was caused by spirits from a malignant plane of existence who were trying to sap her of her energy and health.

She had bad dreams, saw visionary figures that gestured and threatened her. She was the victim of strange rapping sounds in her apartment, mostly on the walls and ceiling of her bedroom.

These three cases demonstrate the symptoms of malicious psychic attack. They were each cured of this trespass by the application of our metaphysical protection program because each of these persons was the target of an intentional wish for destruction which came from another person or persons.

Symptoms of malicious psychic attack

The symptoms of these attacks are:

1. *Unhealthy conditions of unknown origin in the body.* Cure of the physical symptoms is either impossible or very difficult. This is because the exact cause of the illness is *not* physical.

2. *The exercise of discordant influences in the material aspects of life.* Nothing seems to go right in relationships with others. The environment of the individual seems to be one of disharmony, lack of privacy, financial uncertainty, and general instability.

3. *Indirect frustration of intellectual capacity.* Clear thinking is absent. Indecision, the absence of certainty, confusion, and mental wandering are present along with a lack of control over emotions and reactions.

4. *The force of the attack blocks spiritual activity.* The individual seeks divine assistance and deliverance, all to no avail. It seems as though no clear channel to divinity can be established. Prayer is fruitless, meditation is impossible, peace and serenity are absent. The aimlessness of it all starts the final stages of purposeful self-destruction and total negation.

5. *Finally, the individual becomes a passive conductor of nothingness* unable to resist the negative trend of his life. Sooner or later the individual causes decay and bitterness within the lives of other people. The individual becomes a conductor of total hatred, jealousy, pride, and vanity.

The metaphysical protection program

What is the correct way to defend oneself from these malicious psychic attacks? When one is bombarded with the full intention of another, either incarnated or discarnated, to do harm emotionally, mentally, physically, or spiritually, what is the procedure that resists this bombardment? The answer is to *radiate a magnetic force field of protection.*

The best time to begin building your protective force field is before you are being attacked. Then your field can be activated and recharged when you know that a malicious attack is in the making.

Here are the steps in magnetic force field radiation:

1. Prepare yourself as you would for meditation.
2. Take three candles and place them in separate holders.
3. Place a straight chair in the center of the room.
4. Put each lighted candle on the floor around the chair. One should be placed directly in front of you as you sit in the chair and one each at your right side and left side. Then sit in the chair. Extinguish all other light.
5. You are now seated in the center of a "tree" of light, one candle directly in front and one on each side of you. Focus your gaze on the candle directly in front of you.
6. Using the candles as guide points, in your mind's eye, create a force field of multicolored light around your entire body from the tips of your toes to the top of your head.
7. Allow your consciousness to be so keenly aware of this multicolored field that you can recall it to mind at any time and actually see it, in your mind's eye, protecting you from all harm of every kind. Repeat this exercise each day using only the amount of time you need to focus the field and establish it firmly in your mind.

If you are beginning to apply this metaphysical protection theory because you know of a specific psychic attack which is being directed at you, ask another person to work with you, sitting opposite you, to help in focusing the force field. If you cannot ask someone else to help, do your Complete Cosmic Illumination meditation *before* you radiate your magnetic force field of protection so that your psychic forces are evenly distributed.

Outcomes in the three case histories cited

Let's see what happened to the cases mentioned earlier in this chapter.

Miss R.B. asked a friend to sit with her in building her force field. They sat each evening for one entire month. I also advised her to make no mention of her use of metaphysical protection. And she was advised not to discuss her problem with anyone. We didn't want any progress reports to be given to the ladies who were wishing her ill luck.

Sydney G. sat with me several times to make certain he was building the field properly. Then, he went on his own. He noticed results immediately. His business once again became successful, he gave no further thought to his two "special" competitors, and he prospered. He continues to radiate his magnetic force field and attributes the extreme profitability of his business to it.

Sophia used this metaphysical theory and easily dispelled the invasion by discarnate entities that were trying to possess her. She almost always did her Complete Cosmic Illumination meditation before building her force field. The symptoms of malicious psychic attack disappeared within several days and never returned.

An important thing to remember

By radiating a magnetic force field rather than by resisting a specific psychic attack, you will be able to protect yourself from known as well as unknown malicious attacks.

A case of migraine attack

Douglas was tormented by migraine headaches. The attacks had become more acute and more frequent over the course of several years. There didn't seem to be any cause or incident which triggered these attacks. But when they hit, Douglas was incapacitated for two or three days at a time.

He had tried everything. Nothing seemed to work. His wife was concerned. His boss was worried. Douglas had a responsible middle management position in a large architectural firm, and thus was under a great deal of pressure to produce. His work environment was not exactly ideal. Internal political maneuvering was constant and the organizational structure was usually in a state of flux as a result of changed job responsibilities.

"I don't believe any one person is wishing me harm but the entire atmosphere is certainly full of negation," he said during his first session.

"Well, let's combine Complete Cosmic Illumination with metaphysical protection. The Cosmic Illumination will give you strength, calmness and serenity. The metaphysical protection will make it impossible for the malicious thoughts of other people to get at you or influence you in any way," I said.

He agreed to give it a try for a month. During the first month he had only one headache which was one less per month than he had been having. He continued for another month. The second month he had no headaches. He decided to continue into the third month. He had no headaches the third month. Now Douglas radiates the protective force field about twice a week and has not had a migraine headache since that first month—which was two years ago at this writing.

The Case of an Athletic Star

Gail was an amateur tennis star. She came to see me two months before a big tournament. Her main symptom of malicious psychic attack was what she felt were slow reactions to the game in spite of heavy practice and additional coaching. The more her reflexes seemed to slow, the more confused and angry with herself she became.

"Since everyone is expecting me to win, I'm the one to beat. I'm sure that there are several people who are hoping that I don't do well. I understand that you can help me ward off the influence of malevolent thought. I'd like to do that," she said.

We started Gail on the metaphysical protection theory without delay. She was an excellent student and set to work quickly to train herself in radiating her force field. By the time the tournament date had arrived she was in full control of her mental and athletic ability and she was totally confident because of her protective training.

The day of the tournament came and she won handily. She

was calm and confident throughout. "It seemed easy today because of the work I'd been doing prior to this time," she said.

An Antique Dealer's Business Protected

Wilfred was an antique dealer. He decided to use his magnetic force field for protection because his business was turning sour. What had been a thriving, lucrative purchase and resale business was becoming a slow moving, low profit enterprise. In Wilfred's case he felt that several other dealers were combining their cooperative efforts to outbuy and outsell him since he had become the biggest and best in his community. He felt that one dealer in particular was a ringleader in preventing him from making the most of his position and the resources at his command. Several tactical moves had been made by this particular dealer that left Wilfred out in the cold.

Wilfred was a highly motivated person and could mobilize his energy toward a goal with ease. He took up radiation of his magnetic force field without the least hesitation and the multicolored force field began to work wonders for him immediately. The day after he started using the metaphysical protection theory he made three thousand dollars profit in a single sale! By the end of the month his profits had netted him eight thousand dollars.

He was about to purchase a new building, and continue his growth. We asked him to delay his decision for another month to see what else would happen. His profits increased again.

He made the move, purchased the building, and today is one of the most successful antique dealers in his part of the country.

Diagnosis of malicious psychic attack

It isn't always easy to know when you are the victim of a malicious psychic attack. Like other conditions brought on by the mental and emotional energy set loose by other people, true motivation is not always clear. Sometimes it is only during the passage of time that we are able to know for certain that we are a target for negative thinking, aggressive attempts to manipulate our lives for malignant ends, or that we are being victimized by destructive intentions beyond our wildest imagination. It is possible to incur the dislike of another person without even realizing that we have done so.

A psychic attack checklist

It certainly does not harm, but does a great deal of good, to radiate your magnetic force field no matter what may be happening to you. The best protection is a strong field, and time and practice will make your field strong. But, you may wonder if you are the victim of a malicious attack. Following are some questions which you can ask yourself to determine if the clues of an attack appear to be present. If you can answer a high percentage of these questions affirmatively, then the chances of your being a victim of an attack are great. If you can answer only a few affirmatively, the chances of your being a victim at the present time are slight. In the final analysis you will have to be the judge of what is being aimed at you. And you will be the person who can accept only the good, repulse the bad, and triumph over all.

Here are the questions; consider them carefully:

1. Do you always seem to be partially ill with a series of different complaints? Do these physical symptoms leave as mysteriously as they start?
2. Is your doctor at a loss to really find the cause of these minor complaints?
3. Is sharp or recurring pain present in your body along with a feeling of general discomfort?
4. Do new friendships turn bad before they have a chance to get off the ground?
5. Are your old friends losing patience with you or do they forget to include you?
6. Do you find that people are intruding on your privacy?

7. Do you have trouble budgeting your money?

8. Are you spending money on purchases that you regret after you make them?

9. Do you feel as though you'll hardly get through the week, month, or year?

10. Do you sometimes think that unseen forces are at work frustrating your life?

11. Are you aware of the negative course of all events when you read the paper?

12. Do you sometimes wish that people would just stop bothering you?

13. Do you ever wake up with a hazy feeling that never really leaves you all day?

14. Do you have trouble making decisions, even simple ones?

15. Do you feel confused when someone asks you a question?

16. Do you ever wonder where your mind is, or do you have trouble concentrating on what you are doing?

17. Do you lose your temper easily, or suddenly feel sorry for everyone in the world?

18. Do you ever think that God does not care, does not exist, or has overlooked you?

19. Do you have frequent urges to get even with everyone?

20. Do you ever feel like giving up, entirely?

How to reverse malicious psychic attacks

As you train yourself in psychic awareness, your extrasensory capacity will be able to warn you when a malicious psychic attack is being directed at you. You will have an uneasy feeling followed by total discomfort if the attack is successful in getting into your thought. Rather than using your magnetic force field for general protection you can quickly prepare an instrument to repel the bombardment. When you resist a specific attack the charge of that attack returns to the point of origin and brings the malicious energy down on the individual who initiated it.

There is a technique for reversing malicious psychic attacks which causes the discomfort to be experienced by the sender. It is a technique that should be used with the utmost caution and precision since miscalculation can cause an innocent per son to suffer from the returned negation.

THE SIMPLE TECHNIQUE

The technique for reversing malicious psychic attacks is simple. It should be practiced before you attempt to use it because when you need it you'll want it for instant use. You won't have time for long preparations; you'll need it the very moment you find yourself under attack.

Here is the technique for reversing the attack. First place yourself in a calm frame of mind, relax your muscles, and fix your gaze on the most distant point visible to you. Take a deep breath, hold it, and then let it out with a loud plosive sound as though you were expelling the negation itself. Take your next deep breath as though the air for it were coming from the distant point you have fixed your gaze on. *Repeat this entire process several times.*

Next, as you inhale from the distant point see in your mind's eye the person from whom the attack is coming. Feel the negation being drawn to you with each breath you inhale. Then exhale as before with a short plosive sound. This time, however, as you exhale with a plosive sound—and it should be as guttural and deep as possible—*see the negation being sent back to the distant point and back to the person from whom it came.*

The key to this technique is the strength of your visualization and the concentrated sound of rejection which you give as you exhale. The sound should definitely indicate what you are doing. You are ridding yourself of a malicious attack and you are *sending it right back.* You can allow your body to be tense as you exhale because you want to include the entire power and energy of your physical, emotional, mental, and spiritual self to impel the negation right back to its source. Don't allow any deviation in its course. Don't lessen your hold on the negation until you have mentally hurled it right back straight as an arrow. Summon all the psychic energy at your command as you perform this exercise.

How Lorna Overcame Psychic Attack from Her Teacher

Lorna was the target of a malicious psychic attack which was planned and executed with remarkable exactness. Lorna was an art student with talent. She had an argument with Mac, an art instructor, over some artistic concepts with which she was experimenting. The intensity of the disagreement had become so great that she felt obliged to discontinue her lessons with Mac. He unwittingly began directing negative thought at Lorna. He was not wishing her ill as such. He was going over and over the argument, reliving it, and adding to its vehemence.

Lorna began to show the classic symptoms. She had trouble eating and sleeping. Her life was becoming disoriented and disharmonious. She seemed to be fighting with herself. She was confused and felt that nothing could extricate her from her circumstances. She had had enough psychic training to recognize the symptoms. And she realized that the source of her trouble was the negation being thrown off by Mac. So, she invoked the technique for reversing malicious psychic attacks. And it was a good thing that she decided to do it. When she felt negation coming from Mac she repelled it instantly. She did this several times within the course of a week. At the end of the week she got a call from Mac asking to see her. She complied with his request.

"I've been thinking about our disagreement," he said. "The more I try to dislike you or feel that you were entirely wrong, the worse I feel. I'd like to apologize for what happened," he blurted at her.

"Yes, I know it has been difficult for you," Lorna replied. And the two of them became friends again. Lorna explained that she had reversed his psychic invasion. It was a case where the reversal worked for the good of both parties.

A Wife Overcomes a Psychic Attack

Sometimes a reversal of a malicious psychic attack works to the advantage of the individual practicing the reversal technique because the originator of the attack continues to send out the malignant thoughts. Howard was an attorney in private practice. He specialized in divorce cases.

Mrs. Simpson came to him with a difficult case. She wanted to divorce her husband, but Mr. Simpson did not want a divorce; he felt that it would damage his reputation and impede his professional advancement. When Mrs. Simpson told him that she had retained Howard for the purpose of getting a divorce he was enraged. He said that he would not permit it. She would rue the day she got a divorce. He would rather see her dead first. He would rather see himself dead first. He would do everything he could to prevent it. He was in a rage.

Harmony was not present in the Simpson household from that moment on. Mr. Simpson was cruel to his wife. He tried to make her feel guilty. He tried to make her change her mind. He tried to interfere with the work Howard was doing for Mrs. Simpson. He called Howard and threatened him.

Mrs. Simpson quickly realized that she needed counseling of some kind in addition to her legal advice. She decided to join one of our psychic study groups. In the meantime, she worked at radiating a magnetic force field for protection. And, she used the technique for reversing malicious attacks from her husband. Both the metaphysical protection and the reversal worked exceptionally well for her. The more abusive her husband got the more she became calm and certain that her course of action was the correct one. He became more and more distraught as he piled one abuse after another on his wife. Mrs. Simpson simply reversed every attack as easily as water falls from a duck's back. None of it harmed her or caused her the anguish that it certainly brought back upon her husband. Each time he mounted an evil onslaught it was repulsed and he bore the negation within his own heart and mind.

In the end, Mrs. Simpson got her divorce, later remarried, and is quite happy. Mr. Simpson complained to the bitter end and tried to throw several legal blocks in the way of the divorce. All were overcome.

An Exceptional Case of Psychic Attack

Maximilian was a strange case. His adaptation on the technique of reversing malicious psychic attack is not recommended. What he did should be told, because his story demonstrates the tremendous power of negation when it is properly directed and focused.

Maximilian was in his early twenties and was interested in the occult. He had an inventive mind and experimented with hypnosis, mental telepathy, and extrasensory perception.

He came across the idea that there might be a great amount of loose negation in the world. He decided to collect it by using the reversal technique. Maximilian was attracting negation to himself as he inhaled and then he would redirect it—this loose ambivalent negation—at three small ivy plants that he had purchased to be the targets of this negation. Otherwise, he took care of the plants, these three negation targets, in the same way that he took care of three *other* ivy plants that he had purchased at the same time Both sets of plants received the same water and sunshine, the same atmospheric temperature. Yet, as a result of this experiment, he was able to kill the three targeted plants simply by mentally sending malevolent influences to them.

He proved what he had set out to prove, namely, that

through the reversal technique he could gather in evil vibrations and then redirect them, as he exhaled, at some other living thing with the result of death.

The practical ethics of reversing malicious psychic attack

It is obvious that reversing a malicious attack can cause harm to the sender. It is reasonable to assume that misdirected reversal can even harm an innocent bystander, someone who is not a party to the original assault. Only the more advanced psychic should attempt it.

There are alternatives to the reversal method for the less experienced.

The variation of the technique would be:

1. Place yourself in a calm frame of mind.
2. Relax your body and fix your gaze on a distant point.
3. Take a deep breath. As you inhale bring the negation into your body.
4. Exhale with a guttural plosive sound so as to expel the negation.
5. See in your mind's eye, the negation being sent to a *neutral* location such as a deep ocean, a lake or other large body of water, to the north pole, or somewhere out in space.

With this variation you are not turning the evil intention back on the person from whom it came. Instead you are neutralizing it by sending it where it cannot hurt anyone.

This alternative technique can be used also to return a malicious psychic attack which has an unknown origin. It is true that there are evil influences in the universe which are waiting to attach themselves to individuals who will accept them. Just as highly evolved spiritual beings can transmit light and love to the earth plane, so, too, earthbound, or lower level, discarnates can transfer these destructive impulses to those who are ready to accept them.

Any serious student of psychic awareness or cosmic attunement can testify to the importance of practicing protection. Without it, psychic energies can be sapped, awareness can bring in the most nightmarish thoughts, and acute fear. Painful emotions, oppressive distress, and suffocation of the self can also take place in those who move too quickly in psychic awareness. Steady, sound growth of your higher mental abilities takes time and concentrated work. There are no shortcuts. But if you follow the path of your own intuitive insight carefully and slowly, the rewards are great, the experiences satisfying.

How to effect protective conditioning

In addition to radiation of your multicolored force field of protection you can condition your mind and body with protective thoughts.

Protective affirmations said aloud create antidotes to mental malpractice. Included here are several affirmations that condition one against the insults of metaphysical negation. They should be said aloud in order to give them their full strength and power. These affirmations have their greatest protective power if said after a few moments of silence and calm. Then, give them everything you've got. Don't be timid! Stand up and let them really be heard. Use your lung power and your vocal mechanism—and listen as you speak.

Protective affirmation to ward off mental harm

My body is a perfect temple of divine functioning. Every fiber and tissue is working perfectly. Energy from the cosmos and the source of all energies fills my mind and body with perfect attunement. Vicious and malicious thought forms cannot enter my body now or at any time in the future. Health and the full radiance of my multicolored force field are shielding me. Love and harmony are warding off all bodily harm. Balance and bodily attunement have created a wonderful protective radiation. The vibrations of my multicolored force field repel and discharge all destructive influences. I am happy, serene,

*calm, and in perfect control as I affirm my protection
from all harm to my body no matter what its origin may be.*

Protective affirmation to ward off mental harm

*My mind is a clear reflection of divine operation. Every
thought is perfectly formed. The renewing energy from
the cosmos and the source of all energies fills my mind
and body. Vicious and malicious thought forms cannot
enter my mind now or at any time in the future. Health
and the full radiance of my multicolored force field are
shielding me from harm. Love and harmony are warding
off all mental harm. Balance and mental attunement have
created a wonderful protective radiation. The vibrations
of my multicolored force field repel and discharge all
destructive influences. I am happy, serene, calm, and in
perfect control as I affirm my protection from all mental
harm no matter what its origin may be. Confusion, indecision, and discord are entirely dissolved as I move in
the light of mental clarity.*

Protective affirmation to ward off spiritual harm

*My deep spiritual self is a perfect portion of divinity.
My deepest being is working in perfect attunement with
the source of all power, God. Vicious and malicious
thought forms cannot enter my force field now or at any
time in the future. The harmony and full radiance of my
multicolored shield is protecting me from all harm of
every kind. Balance and bodily attunement have created
a wonderful protective radiation. Mental clarity has
added to this protection. Vibrations of my force field
repel and discharge all destructive influences that may
be aimed at my spiritual selfhood. I am happy, serene,
calm, and confident as I affirm protection from all harm
no matter what its origin may be. I affirm that I am protected always by my multicolored force field.*

Protective affirmation to ward off financial disaster

*My every action is a perfect demonstration of divine
creativity. Everything that I become involved in is pros-
pering and will continue to prosper as the power of the
cosmos is regenerated in my life. Vicious and malicious*

thought forms cannot enter my life or its prosperity now or at any time in the future. The full radiance of my multicolored force field is shielding me from all harm. Love and harmony are warding off all financial disaster or lack of any material kind. Balance and attunement have created a wonderful protective radiation. Prosperity is within my being and expresses itself in all that I undertake. The source of all financial gain is protected and shielded from negation of every kind no matter what its origin.

Protective affirmation to ward off disturbing relationships

My relationships with other people are perfect reflections of divine functioning. Every encounter, every conversation is filled with cosmic love and harmony. Vicious and malicious thought forms cannot penetrate my relationships with anyone. The full radiance of my multicolored force field is shielding every expression of love and every contact with another person. Harmony and perfect cosmic attunement are warding off the destructive impulses so that each relationship can grow and bloom into perfect expression. Balance and protection of my loving vibrations are healing and nourishing my relationships. I am in perfect control of my relationships with other people and I am protected from all harm no matter what its origin.

You may want to use one of these affirmations each day before you radiate your magnetic force field. Affirmations are an excellent way to prepare yourself for meditation and prayer as well. Or, perhaps, you will want to use these affirmations as you arise or just before you go to bed each night. Remember to say them out loud, don't just read them over. Hearing them spoken by your own voice will add strength and power to them and they will help condition you for perfect living. As you prepare your interior world through protective thought, you will be preparing your outer world as well. The more often you use these affirmations the more they will be able to assist you in conditioning your protective field for its job of protecting you from unwanted psychic attacks.

Release these affirmations once you've said them. That is, once you've given an affirmation all the energy you can, simply relax again, and forget about it. Once you've done the conditioning there is no need to dwell on it any further. You have set the law into motion and it will work of its own accord. So sit back and take it easy with the full awareness that you have taken the necessary steps and done the required work.

SOME CASE HISTORIES IN POINT

Arthur, aged twenty-eight, had been plagued with bad credit. When he was quite young he had had a car repossessed. This record of nonpayment made it difficult to buy anything on credit. When he had saved a little money, he'd be so anxious to spend it that he'd run right out and buy something frivolous so that his rating never improved.

He had reached the point in life when he needed another car to get to work. So, he decided to use the affirmation to ward off financial difficulty. He amended it a little to include a line or two about saving money which was really the crux of his problem. He needed to have some evidence of "saved" money. For six months he actually recited the affirmation at the top of his lungs in the basement of his home. The basement was the only place where he could be *that* loud. All the while, he saved money, regularly, from each pay check. He purchased savings bonds with the money so he had something tangible to show for his work. At the end of that time he cashed the bonds in and had enough for a down payment on a new car. Meanwhile, the strict budgeting caused by the savings plan had made it easy for Arthur and his wife to pay their bills promptly. Their credit rating improved and he had no trouble getting the car.

Erma used the affirmation to ward off mental harm. Some days, as she described it, it was all she could do to get up. She felt "undone" most of the time. She knew the cause of this feeling was mental. In time this affirmation not only braced her, it gave her a zip and dash for living that was contagious. Everyone noticed it, including her early morning milkman.

That's how early she was getting up. She told him that she was using an affirmation. "You mean you just talk to yourself?" he asked.

"That's right," she said, "it's better than vitamin pills."

It may not be pleasant to admit that there are harmful influences in the world. But when we recognize that they do exist it makes it easy to deal with them. And it is almost axiomatic that dealing with negation and triumphing over it *is* "better than taking vitamin pills."

Exercises to perform

1. *Create the opposite symptoms*—Take each of the symptoms of malicious psychic attack and concentrate your attention on the creation of the opposite, i.e., positive thought forms.

   a. Focus your attention on the creation of a healthy body.

   b. Focus your attention on the creation of a harmonious environment.

   c. Focus your attention on the creation of clear intellectual operation.

   d. Focus your attention on obtaining divine assistance in your life.

   e. Focus your attention on the creation of total being.

2. *Change the colors of your force field*—Improve the multicolored hues of your force field by allowing it to change color as you meditate on radiating it. Go through the entire range of colors. Then create a rainbow of color emanating from your heart center. Then allow the colors to emanate from your pelvic area, the abdomen, the chest, the throat, and the forehead.

3. *Neutralize your own negative thoughts*—Neutralize your own negative thoughts by sending them to a body of water, out into space, or to an uninhabited place such as the north pole or deep in a jungle.

4. *Help a friend be protected from malicious psychic attack*—Teach this method of radiating a multicolored force field to a friend of yours who is in need. When you have free time, assist your friend further by helping to build the force field of protection. Try to meet once or twice a week to work together on this project of self-help. Allow your friend to help you build your radiation also. Think of yourselves as partners, as conductors of positive protection from malicious psychic attacks of all kinds.

5. *Neutralize your own negative discharge*—When you feel yourself harboring negation, harm, jealousy, or ill will toward any other human being, send that thought to a neutral place for dissolution. Block any harmful thoughts you may be sending out to anyone else and simply place them in a neutral position so that they do not go out as psychic attacks. In this way you will be preventing anyone else from reversing an attack back onto you as the unwitting source of a negative mental discharge.

Points to remember from this chapter

1. Negative thought forms can be just as powerful and effective as positive thought forms.

2. The various symptoms of malicious psychic attack have been listed for your reference.

3. Metaphysical protection can ward off malicious psychic attack by radiating a magnetic force field of protection.

4. Malicious psychic attacks can be reversed by exhaling them and sending them back to the person or persons who originated them.

5. The ethics of reversing malicious psychic attack includes alternative methods of sending the attacks to a neutral place for dissolution.